The Natural Survival of Work

The Natural Survival of Work

Job Creation and Job Destruction in a Growing Economy

Pierre Cahuc and André Zylberberg

translated by William McCuaig

The MIT Press
Cambridge, Massachusetts
London, England

This work has been published with support from the Ministère français chargé de la culture—Centre national du livre.

MIT Press books may be purchased at special quantity discounts for business or sales promotional use. For information, please email special_sales@mitpress. mit.edu or write to Special Sales Department, The MIT Press, 55 Hayward Street, Cambridge, MA 02142.

This book was set in Sabon by SNP Best-set Typesetter Ltd., Hong Kong. Printed and bound in the United States of America.

Library of Congress Cataloging-in-Publication Data

Cahuc, Pierre.
[Chômage, fatalité ou nécessité. English]
The natural survival of work : job creation and job destruction in a growing economy / Pierre Cahuc and André Zylberberg ; translated by William McCuaig.
    p.   cm.
Includes bibliographical references and index.
Translation of: Le chômage, fatalité ou nécessité.
ISBN-13: 978-0-262-03357-2 (alk. paper)
ISBN-10: 0-262-03357-7 (alk. paper)
1. Unemployment—France. 2. Manpower policy—France. I. Zylberberg, André. II. Title.

HD5775.C29513   2006
331.12'0420944—dc22
                                                          2006044975

10 9 8 7 6 5 4 3 2 1

to Manon, Marie-Christine, Ana, Arthur, Jeanne, and Paul

Contents

Acknowledgments

This work owes much to the encouragement, and even more to the perspicacious comments and critiques, of our friends, colleagues, and editors, who have generously devoted a good deal of their time to reading and rereading our text. In particular, we thank Yann Algan, Daniel Baroin, Sophie Berlin, Jean Domingues Dos Santos, Manon Domingues Dos Santos, Françoise Ducrocq-Curdel, Olivier Galland, Bernard Gazier, Pierre Granier, Pierre Hallier, Marie-Christine Jobic, Hubert Kempf, Francis Kramarz, Fabien Postel-Vinay, Nicolas Riboud-Sainclair, Isabelle Robin, Jean-Marc Robin, Bernard Salanié, and Perrine Simon-Nahum. We are also indebted to John Covell, our editor at the MIT Press, the production team at the Press, and William McCuaig, translator, for their outstanding cooperation, effectiveness, and professionalism.

The Natural Survival of Work

Introduction

Many countries, especially in continental Europe, have been suffering from chronic unemployment for almost three decades. Failure to understand the true nature of the labor market is, in part, responsible for this situation. The fact is that only recently have the best-informed researchers and experts come to realize that this market functions in a very strange way, simultaneously creating and destroying a considerable number of jobs. Every working day in the United States 90,000 jobs disappear and an equal number are created; and a similar process has long been at work in all the industrialized countries. This discovery has radically altered the way we think about the functioning of the labor market. A related discovery is that this process does not have much to do with the process of globalization. It is, however, closely related to the way in which market economies create wealth. Without this phenomenon of "creative destruction" we would simply never have experienced growth.[1] Growth is not some miraculous manna that only falls from the skies thanks to a handful of revolutionary inventions, like electricity in the recent past or the new information and communication technologies of today. Innovations do propel growth. But they cannot be put into operation, and promote constant growth in all sectors and trades, without this incessant process of job destruction and job creation. This process brings material progress, but it also entails unemployment and conspicuous inequalities.

Yet debates about what policies should be adopted in order to counter unemployment and inequality are virtually untouched by this reality. Most of the time, especially in continental Europe, they are grounded on an erroneous conception of the labor market, in which jobs are supposed to last forever and every instance of job destruction is seen as an abnormal, dramatic event, to be avoided at any cost. For that matter, in periods of rising unemployment, most of the news about jobs concerns mass layoffs, although these involve fewer than 10 percent of persons leaving their jobs in all OECD countries. Those in power and in the media, subjected to this constant pressure, perhaps believe that they are doing the right thing when they concentrate only on this facet of the situation. Clearly, we should not abandon all interest in the fate of those affected by mass layoffs. But when those in power and the media focus on a very marginal component of the labor market instead of considering this market in its totality, they run the risk of putting inefficient and unjust institutional mechanisms in place. We shall see that, in order to create an efficient and just system, it is vital to change this way of thinking. We have to recognize the inexorable, massive, and—this term may startle readers—*useful* character not only of job destruction but also of unemployment. We must stop treating job destruction as an accident, and unemployed persons as victims or bearers of guilt. Job destruction is indispensable for growth, and looking for a job is a socially useful activity, which ought to be remunerated for that reason.

In many countries, the difficulty of combating unemployment derives from an incapacity to accept the inexorable and useful character of job destruction. In this respect, France is emblematic. François Mitterrand caused a sensation in 1993 when he declared that "everything had been tried" when it came to unemployment. It is true that a very wide range of strategies has been adopted: increased public expenditure, then its opposite; reduction of the length of the work week; substantial utilization of early retirement; an increase in the number of high school graduates; the development of public works projects; the promotion of entry-level jobs; reductions in payroll taxes; and so on. But the truth is that when it comes to unemployment, nothing has been tried *seriously* because, especially in President Mitterrand's country, nothing has been genuinely *evaluated*. Each new government arrives with its own plans for reform and puts them in place with more or less determination. Then another government comes along and brings in its own new reforms, quite often retaining a good portion of the previous ones, and without really knowing what actually works. For thirty years we have witnessed a merry-go-round of measures without any accumulation of knowledge about their effects. France is suffering, in this regard, from an authentic democratic deficit: there exists no independent agency equipped with adequate resources for evaluating the government's interventions in the labor market. As things stand, any evaluation of policies to battle unemployment takes place essentially under the aegis of the government's "communication strategy."

Paradoxically, this democratic deficit politicizes positions quite uselessly. In the absence of cumulative knowledge, precise facts, and soundly premised deliberation, the debate has become ever more polarized between, on the one hand, supporters of "flexibility," hostile to any action by the government, and on the other, supporters of government intervention of every kind, with their scattershot proposals for a high minimum wage, a ban on firing, generous unemployment insurance and welfare payments, ever greater public-sector hiring—all of this accompanied by a large budgetary deficit in order to stimulate demand. The former are seen as arguing principally in terms of efficiency, the latter in terms of social justice and equity. This Manichean polarity is based, for the most part, on ignorance of the lessons to be learned from economic analysis, a discipline that has made impressive advances in recent years, thanks in particular to the utilization of huge databases.

Take the example of the minimum wage. We will see that the theory predicts that raising it can, in certain circumstances, increase employment, but that it can also, in other circumstances, reduce employment. Assessment of the effects of the minimum wage is therefore, in the end, a practical, "empirical" problem, which can be resolved, or at any rate clarified, by appropriate evaluative procedures. Such procedures do exist. They are based on experiments or surveys comprising hundreds, thousands, or in some cases even millions of observations. The methods by which these data can be processed have today achieved a degree of reliability such that their results are infinitely more representative than what can be learned from an interview with a CEO, a trade unionist, a teacher, a politician, a striker, or an angry consumer. Our grasp of social phenomena is, in fact, profoundly influenced by our own position in society. Knowledge of the facts and how they are statistically processed is the best defense against autosuggestion and demagogic speechifying. The truth is much more to be found in the inhuman aridity of figures and graphs than in "live" interviews heard on the radio or seen on television.

Without true knowledge of the facts, and without objective, independent evaluation, any effort to diagnose the functioning of the labor market is not much different from taking a political stance. Thus you are on the left if you assert that increases in the minimum wage are favorable to employment, and on the right if you assert the opposite. Such posturing is absurd; worse, it reinforces a form of intellectual laziness. You can still be on the left and wish to maintain a high minimum wage, all the while knowing that the cost of labor (often) hinders employment. But that obliges you, first, to accept reality—not the easiest thing to do— and then to come up with measures capable of reducing the cost of labor that also stay within the bounds of reality—which is perhaps even less easy.

Contrary to what is far too widely believed, economic analysis has made much progress in the study of employment and unemployment. The age when there were as many opinions as there were economists has passed. On a great many questions, knowlege is very soundly established, and is the object of a broad consensus on an international scale. Yet this knowledge base is still largely unknown. This book aims to present the state of our knowledge to the general public, and to derive lessons from it for improving the functioning of the labor market. The first two chapters reveal both the extent and the necessity of the process of job destruction and job creation. They highlight the astonishing reactivity of labor markets, which makes the majority of industrialized countries capable of destroying, but also of creating, large numbers of jobs in a very short space of time. In this world in perpetual transformation, the work demanded by firms is not a fixed quantity that can be rationed out. Thus the diminution of the number of participants in the labor force due to the aging of the population may result in a rise—and not a fall—in unemployment; the reduction of the work week can just as well destroy jobs as create them; and finally, an influx of immigrants does not automatically lead to a rise in unemployment.

With that background filled in, chapters 3 and 4 dissect the logic of job creation. Wages evidently play an overriding part: they must be high enough to make work attractive, but not so high as to act as a deterrent to firms. This finding is illustrated by an abundance of studies that throw fresh light on the role of the minimum wage, the impact of reducing payroll taxes on low wages, and the consequences of fiscal policies. Chapters 5 and 6 are devoted to the management of the risks generated by the great magnitude of shifts in employment and in the workforce. In this area, unemployment insurance and the regulation of layoffs have an essential part to play. To be efficient and equitable, they must be managed according to certain rules, simple ones in principle. Nevertheless, we show that these rules are seldom applied in countries in which unemployment and inefficiency in the labor market are persistent. Finally, chapters 7 and 8 deal with education, training, and employment policy. Universal education, lifelong training, and jobs in the public and non-profit sector are often presented as miracle remedies in the battle against unemployment. Evaluation of public policy contradicts these received ideas. When it comes to training and employment policy, the road to hell, alas, is paved with good intentions.

To accept this knowledge base does not oblige one to declare allegiance to any sort of "groupthink," for although the facts are effectively straightforward, there is always a spectrum of policies that may be adopted in response to them, and they do not all offer us the same future.

1

Ninety Thousand Jobs Destroyed Every Day

The 15 percent rule

In the United States, every year, 21.5 million jobs disappear. In France, during the same period, 2.3 million jobs disappear. If you look at it on a daily basis, the extent of the carnage is striking: every working day, the United States loses 90,000 jobs and France loses 10,000 jobs. Ninety thousand per day—that is every job in Santa Cruz-Watsonville (California); it is 49 jobs per minute. At that rate, there won't be a single job left in the United States in less than seven years! Figures like these could easily convince anyone who is of good faith—but not well informed—of the inevitable end of work. Fortunately, this perspective only tells half the story, and the other half is just as interesting. It can be summarized in a short sentence: every day, the United States *creates* 90,000 jobs, while France *creates* 10,000 jobs.[1]

All in all, the truth is a lot more daunting than the banal end of work so often predicted. The quantities of jobs destroyed and created are gigantic, and year in and year out, they manage to offset each other. Thus between 1990 and 2003, in the United States the average quarterly *net* growth of private employment, measured by the difference between jobs destroyed and created, was 370,000 jobs, or 0.3 percent of total private employment. During this period the private sector of the U.S. economy destroyed 7.7 percent of its jobs every quarter . . . and created 8 percent, so that it provided a *net* growth in private employment of 0.3 percent per quarter, which is meager compared to the 8 percent of jobs created or to the 7.7 percent of jobs destroyed.[2]

Full awareness of the extent of job creation and destruction is recent. Only since the end of the 1980s have economists had available precise data covering sufficiently long periods. The *simultaneous* presence of such high numbers of jobs created and destroyed surprised them, and caused them to pay homage to one of their illustrious predecessors, the Austrian Joseph Schumpeter, who, though he had only skimpy data to work with, had grasped as early as the 1940s that this process, which he called "creative destruction," was the principal driver of growth, but also one of the principal causes of unemployment.[3] Another surprise for researchers was the discovery that these movements in employment were substantially identical in all industrialized countries.[4] To put it in a nutshell, we may speak appropriately of a "15 percent rule," which may be stated as follows: *on the national scale, around 15 percent of jobs disappear every year, and every year around 15 percent of new jobs come into being.*

In light of what has just been said, the amount of attention paid and the indulgence granted to several writers who have proclaimed the inevitable disappearance of work are surprising. Viviane Forrester states, in *The Economic Horror* (1996), that "job creation" is "a notoriously empty and utterly blighted formula, [but] nevertheless inescapable, because no longer lying on the subject might soon mean no longer believing in it, and having to wake up and find oneself in a nightmare belonging to neither sleep nor even waking fantasy."[5] She is, on the face of it, taking only job destruction into account and forgetting job creation. Jeremy Rifkin displays the same blindness in *The End of Work*, which appeared in 1995 in the United States and was a hit for its publishers. His 400-plus pages, bolstered by a multitude of examples of firms destroying jobs, "demonstrate" that the death knell has sounded for work. Since the United States alone destroys 90,000 jobs per day, it isn't hard for anyone to recount dozens of stories about businesses failing or slashing their workforces. Industrialized economies do indeed destroy many jobs, but they also create a great many, and by an irony of history, during the five years that followed the appearance of these two books, job creation markedly outstripped job destruction, not just in the United States, where that is the normal pattern, but also in most developed countries. All the data we have supply not the slightest inkling of proof for these catastrophist pseudo-theories. So how to account for the reception given such false prophets, and their success? Their depiction of an apocalypse probably strikes the imagination of readers directly and effortlessly. Compared to that, dealing with a nuanced array of pros and cons quickly starts to look like a chore both tiresome and, in the nature of things, endlessly debatable. Moreover, job destructions are often synonymous with personal drama. Distress and anger can easily be displayed for effect, whereas job creations are mostly diffused phenomena, and as a general rule there is nothing to display. Harping on millenarian fears— and the fear of the end of work is one of these—will always have wider resonance than a serious study, documented with figures, that arrives at unspectacular and not always clear-cut conclusions.

The fact is that we are not witnessing the disappearance of work, but rather its unceasing recomposition. This recomposition is massive. We will see that, in essence, growth depends on it. But it also creates unemployment, inequality, and exclusion. The process of job creation and destruction is thus at the center of the great economic and social problems of our time. It is still largely unknown. No doubt this is why the most implausible notions about the future of work, the role of globalization, stock-market-driven layoffs, rising inequality, and even increasing pauperization can thrive. To work out an efficient and equitable way of regulating the labor market demands an understanding of why this process of job creation and destruction is indispensable.

How jobs "spill over"

Having registered the fact that the volume of jobs created was counterbalancing that of jobs destroyed, year by year, economists expected that further investigation would confirm the common-sense intuition that the jobs destroyed must be coming principally from sectors in decline, and that the counterbalance of jobs created must be coming from expanding sectors. But they had the further surprise of discovering that these movements of creation and destruction were taking place simultaneously within the *same* sectors. Take the example of the textile and pharmaceutical industries in France between 1990 and 1996. The former heads the list of sectors in decline, while the latter is a "leading edge" sector.

Given that, on a national scale, job creation more or less balances job destruction, the assumption was that a sector like textiles destroys jobs while the pharmaceutical sector creates them. Table 1.1 shows us that reality is more subtle.

Between 1990 and 1996, the declining textile industry created almost as many jobs every year as the expanding pharmaceutical and perfume industry (7.1 percent and 7.3 percent, respectively). Textiles are in decline because, *every year*, they destroy appreciably more jobs than they create, whereas pharmaceuticals/perfumes are expanding because, *every year*, they destroy fewer jobs, by a small margin, than they create. But it is never the case that one industry does nothing but create jobs or does nothing but destroy them. On the contrary, all sectors are always busy creating *and* destroying numerous jobs. Decline is a cumulative phenomenon over a long period, in which, every year, job destruction materially outstrips job creation.

In other words, a declining sector does indeed shed jobs while expanding sectors are adding them, but this phenomenon takes place slowly. Over the course of a year, the great majority of jobs destroyed in the textile sector are replaced by jobs in the textile sector. For example, in France's Nord–Pas-de-Calais region, factories specializing in the making of traditional textiles have continually been reducing their workforces during the last two decades. But from the beginning of the 1990s, the production of "technical" textiles based on synthetic fibers and utilized by medical personnel, in construction, and in certain sports, among other things, has experienced strong, sustained growth. Today a

Table 1.1
Job Creation and Destruction in France in Textiles and Pharmaceuticals (Annual Average, 1990–1996)

Sector	Creations	Destructions	Net growth*
Textiles	7.1%	11.4%	−4.3%
Pharmaceuticals and perfumes	7.3%	6.2%	+1.1%

* Net growth represents the difference between creation and destruction.
Source: Richard Duhautois, "Les réallocations d'emplois en France sont-elles en phase avec le cycle?," table 4.

genuine "valley" of technical textiles comprising more than 150 companies has grown up around the city of Lille. Some of the jobs destroyed by traditional textiles have spilled over into technical textiles. This is a "law" that, once again, holds good in all the industrialized countries. Studies carried out to date indicate that the bulk of the criss-cross movements of job destruction and creation—what economists call job reallocation—takes place not between different sectors, but among businesses belonging to the *same* sector. If we divide industrial production in France into 600 different sectors, the movements of jobs between sectors represent less than 20 percent of the total number of reallocations.[6]

Creative destruction and growth

Everyone rejoices at the announcement of new jobs being created. But the announcement of a layoff repels and mortifies most of our fellow citizens. They see it as a sign of the failure of the market economy. For some, it even proves the failure of capitalism. In light of what we now know about the extent of job creation and destruction and the relative balance between these two movements, it becomes even more awkward to defend capitalism. Its defenders now have to account for the fact that in the same country, the same sector, even the same subsector, capitalism has to devour just about as many jobs as it generates. If the number of jobs created in a particular sector is approximately equal to that of jobs destroyed, would it not be possible to keep most people on in the firm that already employs them, and so avoid all the suffering that goes along with restructuring? This question already preoccupied Joseph Schumpeter more than sixty years ago, and he proposed an answer which recent research has confirmed: *the main source of growth is a process of creative destruction.*

To follow this line of reasoning, you must first realize that all jobs are exposed to endless innovation, marginal or invasive, which has the ultimate goal of improving their productivity, that is to say, their capacity to produce.[7] For example, the introduction of bar codes freed checkout clerks from having to enter prices manually. In an hour of work, a checkout clerk can get through two or three times as many grocery carts as before, thanks to bar codes. That clerk's productivity has thus been multiplied two or three times. All sectors of the economy are permanently exposed to major or minor innovations, and to changes in their environment.

In this setting, firms have to innovate ceaselessly in order to improve, or simply maintain, their profitability, by trying new methods of production and personnel management, or by trying to sell new products. Some innovations bear fruit, others fail. Firms that have the ability and the luck to adopt the right innovations take market share away from others. It is from these trials and these errors that increased productivity originates, and the corollary of increased productivity is that jobs are reallocated between firms, and also within firms. In this sense, job destructions are actually an expression of the creation of extra value: jobs are destroyed in a firm because other, more productive ones are being created in that firm or in other firms. Such is the logic of the process of creative destruction. Another way of stating Schumpeter's conclusion is to say that we would collectively have much less wealth without the incessant movement of job creation and destruction. Prosperity arises from the reallocation of jobs.

Thus, with the availability today of rich data provided by surveys covering long periods, recent research shows that innovations improve productivity mainly thanks to the process of creative destruction. To a large extent, this process takes place within existing firms,[8] but that is far from being the case every time. The combination of job reallocation between different firms, the appearance of new firms, and the disappearance of older firms explains half the growth in productivity of the North American manufacturing sector in the 1980s and 1990s.[9] The numbers are more striking still in the retail sales sector. Since the end of the 1980s this sector has undergone a revolution linked to advances in information technology. This revolution involves the use of bar codes, but also the immediate transmission of all purchases made at the cash register to the inventory managers, who can in turn adjust their stock very rapidly. In the United States, over the decade 1987 to 1997, reallocations between firms accounted for more than 80 percent of the growth in productivity of this sector. In other words, less than 20 percent of the growth in productivity in retail sales came from reorganizations within the *same* company.[10]

The fragility of firms

The studies we have just cited do not tell us why the reorganization of jobs within existing companies has only a modest part to play in the increased productivity of certain sectors. Ricardo Caballero and Mohamad Hammour have focused particularly on this question.[11] Their main conclusion is that the way a business functions is always highly specific. Every firm is a complex piece of alchemy, a culture molded by time and including technical know-how, the interweave of not-always-explicit personal and collective ties, and its own rules and customs for organizing the work and making decisions. This amalgam is, to a large extent, proper to each firm, and works well only within that particular entity. A firm is more like a system composed of irreversible links between certain of its elements than a collection of undifferentiated individuals and machines that one could remodel at will. When a technological innovation occurs, or when the competitive circumstances change, certain firms, or certain units within the same firm, are not capable of adapting, because the degree of specificity of their internal relations is too strong. They disappear, in part or in whole, while at the same time better-adapted firms or plants appear.

The experience of air transportation is instructive on this point. The terrorist attacks of 11 September 2001 caused the rapid decline of a sector that was already hurting. Most of the bigger companies have reduced their fleets, while others—like Swissair or Sabena—have simply disappeared. Yet between summer 2001 and summer 2002 the six largest "low-cost" carriers (Ryanair, Easyjet, Buzz, Virgin Express, Go, and Bmibaby) increased their passenger numbers on average by 48 percent. For an economist, a low-cost company is nothing more than a traditional company *plus* some "innovations": the low-cost companies have increased the number of seats per plane, offer no on-board service, do not maintain extensive networks, often own just one type of aircraft, have minimal administrative structures, often use small airports not served by traditional carriers, and so on. The sum of these innovations leads to the productivity of work in a low-cost company being manifestly greater than that in a traditional carrier. Thus, in April 2002 there were on average 227 employees per aircraft at Air France and 254 at British Airways, but these figures fell to 76 at Virgin Express, 68 at Easyjet, and 36 at Ryanair. The low-cost companies have created jobs—internally and in the whole air transportation sector—while the traditional companies have destroyed jobs. For example, in Europe in 2001, 30 percent of the hires of pilots were done by low-cost carriers, whereas these carriers represented, at that time, scarcely 11 percent of European passenger traffic.[12]

The process of creative destruction occurred to the benefit of the low-cost companies and to the detriment of the traditional carriers. The latter have indeed tried to react, in some cases by creating their own low-cost offshoots, but with mixed success. For that matter, industry experts take the view that the traditional carriers will never really succeed in competing with the low-cost companies, because the organization of a traditional company is too highly specific for it to become, or to generate, a low-cost company. Leo Mullin, who was at the helm of Delta, America's third largest airline, put it humorously: "a dinosaur's baby will always be a dinosaur."[13] When all is said and done, the low-cost companies will have raised the productivity of the air transportation sector considerably. And, barring a fresh catastrophe, more and more people will travel by airplane (for it is becoming cheaper on average), more and more new airlines will start up (for destinations that aren't profitable with traditional carriers become so with low-cost companies), and the jobs will have been redistributed within the air transportation sector. The process of creative destruction will have accomplished its task.

Air transportation is not an isolated example. All the OECD countries are affected by a high rate of creation and disappearance of *firms*. Eric Bartelsman, Stefano Scarpetta, and Fabiano Schivardi have found that around 10 percent of firms disappear, on average, every year in every country of the OECD.[14] Quite obviously, as with the destruction of jobs, destructions of firms are generally compensated for by creations: each year the number of businesses created represents 10 percent of existing firms.

Movements of jobs and manpower

The fact that the efficiency of every firm is the result of a specific alchemy sheds light on another surprising phenomenon: every working day, while 90,000 jobs are being destroyed in the United States, 250,000 people lose or leave their jobs . . . and a little more than 250,000 find a job; in France, while 10,000 jobs are being destroyed, 30,000 people lose or leave their jobs . . . and 30,000 people find a job. This phenomenon reflects a general tendency: in the industrialized countries, reallocations of manpower are from two to three times more numerous than reallocations of jobs. This gap arises, in the first place, from workers quitting voluntarily. In France, every working day, 6,000 persons quit and 4,000 go into retirement. These departures do not necessarily cause jobs to be destroyed. For the most part, they cause employers to hire new individuals. Thus bosses are not the only ones responsible for rotation in the workforce; a significant percentage of reallocations of manpower results from the free choice of wage-earners. The labor market is one of the areas in which freedom of movement is expressed in a democratic society.

But it is also the extreme specificity of each firm that requires movements of manpower of such dimensions. In following 1,669 French firms between 1987 and 1990, John Abowd, Patrick Corbel, and Francis Kramarz have highlighted the size, and the source, of this phenomenon.[15] They demonstrate that the management of manpower is marked by a considerable number of *simultaneous* hires and departures. On average, a firm that creates one job does so by hiring three persons, while two others leave. More surprisingly, these authors have also found that firms that destroy jobs continue to hire. On average, the loss of a position results from two hires and three departures. This study strongly confirms that each successful hire is the outcome of a process of trial and error, for every job has its specificity, which depends not only on the tasks demanded but also on a network of personal relationships, the culture of the firm, its location, and a host of factors that may suit some people and repel others. These factors are not all immediately apparent, and it is largely for this reason that trial periods and hires on fixed-term contract are so widely utilized. Growth is thus the outcome of a joint process of job creation and destruction, and movements of manpower. This joint process is massive. It reflects both the choices of firms and the freedom of movement of workers.

Is unemployment necessary?

The movements of jobs and manpower transform many workers into unemployed persons[16] who have to look for new jobs. The activity of looking is essential for the economy to function well, because it allows destroyed jobs to give rise to new, more productive jobs. The hunt for a job—or to put it another way, unemployment—is thus an indispensable cog in the process of creative destruction and growth.

Yet, while all industrialized countries are much alike in terms of job creation and destruction—every year around 15 percent of jobs are created and 15 percent of jobs are destroyed—they vary considerably in terms of unemployment. For example, in 2004, France posted a rate of unemployment of 9.6 percent, while Sweden leveled out at 6.4 percent, the United States did better with 5.5 percent, and the Netherlands better still with 4.7 percent. When the situation deteriorates, the gaps persist. The rate of unemployment in the United States can reach 7 percent, and that of France 12 percent. How do we explain the persistence of such large gaps? Many analysts point to demographic factors. According to them, there are too many people who want to work (young people, women, immigrants), whereas the number of jobs on offer is stagnant and the age of retirement is being raised. We will see in the next chapter that this view does not have any solid basis. On the contrary, it is the industrialized countries with the most robust increase in the working-age population that have the lowest rates of unemployment.

An explanation favored by many lays the blame on sluggish growth. From this angle, unemployment rises when growth "fails to arrive," but when it finally does, unemployment will certainly go down. This notion is, at best, a restatement of the obvious. The sluggishness of growth is not the *cause* of rising unemployment, and the return of growth is not the *cause* of falling unemployment. In actuality, growth and unemployment are *jointly* determined by the process of job creation and destruction. More precisely, it is the manner in which each country manages this process that results in that country having more or less growth, and more or fewer unemployed persons. If countries diverge persistently in terms of growth and unemployment, it is because their labor markets are organized differently. The cost of labor, social security, the overall concept of unemployment insurance and public help for job-seekers, procedures for hiring and firing, public spending on employment, and the system for providing training vary from one country to another. The effects of such differences have been widely studied in the last decade, and these studies converge on the increasingly robust conclusion that gaps in the rate of unemployment observed among OECD countries arise in large measure from differences in the organization of their labor markets.

Does globalization make unemployment worse?

For many, globalization is the main reason that jobs are destroyed. As well, it is believed to destroy many more jobs than it creates. The reasoning that leads to this conclusion is simple, and instantly convincing. It can be summed up as follows: since the cost of unskilled labor is very low in developing countries, we cannot compete with them in markets for products that require a lot of unskilled labor to make. So we import these products instead of making them ourselves, and that causes a great many unskilled jobs to be destroyed here at home. Of course, we export high-value-added products derived from leading-edge technologies to the developing countries, but making them requires little manpower (which must anyway be highly skilled) and plenty of capital in the form of machinery and equipment. In other words, our exports are produced with little labor, while our imports are produced with a lot of labor. In this setting, the final balance of jobs depending on international trade will be highly negative as far as we are concerned.

In reality, there are a number of reasons to doubt this analysis, and thus to doubt its conclusions. In the first place, it is not so certain that our export products are made with much capital and little manpower. In 1955 Wassily Leontief caused a sensation by showing, with the numbers to prove it, that the United States was exporting goods that were clearly more labor-intensive than the goods that it was importing, to the point that the community of economists coined the term "the

Leontief paradox."[17] Investigations carried out since then have tended to confirm his result, but also to show that the exports of the developed countries were, in fact, intensive in skilled labor. In the second place, the volume of trade with developing countries remains very modest. In 1999, for the 15 countries of the European Union, imports of manufactured products coming from developing countries represented no more than 7.8 percent of their total imports of manufactured goods (for products of this type, 62 percent of imports in the EU come from within the EU). Overall, the vision of globalization as a destroyer of jobs starts to look less solid than the initial line of reasoning made it seem, and only from empirical studies, which abound in this domain, is it possible to get a clearer picture.

One of the most commonly used ways of assessing the effects of globalization on employment is called the "balance of jobs" method. The principle is simple. Many surveys supply us with regular information on the links between the volume of production and the volume of employment in all sectors of the economy. The same sources also inform us about the volumes of exports and imports specific to every sector. On that basis, it becomes possible to estimate, for each sector, how many jobs are "destroyed" by imports and how many jobs are "created" by exports. The difference between jobs created by exports and jobs destroyed by imports forms the "balance of jobs" for that sector. If it is negative, that means that international trade has destroyed more jobs than it has created for the sector in question. The converse is true if the balance of jobs turns out positive. Finally, the total of the sectoral balances forms the balance of jobs for the whole country.

This exercise was carried out by Stéphane Guimbert and François Lévy-Bruhl for the French economy between 1978 and 1997.[18] They find that over the first twelve years, between 1978 and 1990, France's balance of jobs was in the red by about 450,000 units, which represents around 3 percent of employment in the non-agricultural private sector. In other words, international trade was responsible for the net loss of around 40,000 jobs per year over this period, a loss which affected skilled labor just as much as it did unskilled labor. Additionally, not all sectors were hit equally hard. For example, over the twelve years 1978 to 1990, international trade cost industry 541,000 jobs, and textiles 116,000 jobs, but spawned 179,000 jobs in the agriculture and food sector.

The picture changes completely for the period 1990 to 1997. The balance of jobs is now in the *black* by about 491,000 units; even more surprisingly, all sectors and all categories of manpower, skilled and unskilled, get the benefit of this surplus. To put it another way, foreign trade put a brake on the decline of industrial jobs instead of accelerating it. Even more surprisingly, the balance of jobs of foreign trade in the textile sector was also in (modest) surplus by 2,000 units, although this sector lost 144,000 jobs overall for the period. Once again, international trade slowed rather than accelerated the shrinkage of jobs in this sector. To all appearances, France began to adapt better to globalization from the start of the 1990s.

One of the striking things this study of France tells us is that globalization does not systematically cause more job loss than job creation there; over twenty years, it seems to be more or less neutral. Note as well that these results cover the entire range of countries with which France has trade relations. Within this range, trade with developing countries plays a very minor part. So to assign trade with these countries a leading role in the degradation of the employment situation is a position that fails to withstand scrutiny on both counts.[19]

The stock market versus employment?

On 20 June 2001, four members of the French National Assembly, the equivalent of the House of Representatives in the United States, submitted a draft bill, the preamble of which begins: "In September 1999 the management of the Michelin group announced an increase in the group's quarterly profits of 20 percent, along with the layoff of 7,500 wage-earners. In the wake of this announcement, the share price of the tire maker rose by 12 percent." Their bill therefore aimed to impose drastic penalties on firms that reduce their workforce during periods when they are making a profit. In short, they wanted to prevent "stock-market-driven" layoffs. This bill did not go forward, but the law on "social modernization" that passed on 17 January 2002 under the left-wing government of Lionel Jospin included a "Michelin amend-ment" forcing employers to negotiate an agreement to reduce working time before engaging in mass layoffs. This amendment was dropped at the instigation of the right-wing Raffarin government on 5 December 2002.

This perception of layoffs as driven by the stock market, a perception amply relayed in the media, rests on a very simple argument: a good way to prove that a firm is well run is to chop several hundred or several thousand jobs, at a time when profits are strong. By doing that, the firm sends a "signal" to the financial markets that its sole management goal is to maximize shareholder satisfaction. We note in passing that this sig-naling strategy would be even more powerful if firms were to be penal-ized financially when they cut their workforce. To shed jobs while making profits, and even pay a penalty for doing so, would in this view be interpreted very favorably indeed by the financial markets. During the last decade, this theory of stock-market-driven layoffs has been the focus of a number of very thorough studies (most of them carried out by American researchers, since this theory attracts a certain amount of support in the United States too), but none of these studies succeeds in confirming it.

The most comprehensive one is probably that of Henry Farber of Princeton University and Kevin Hallock of the University of Illinois.[20] They compiled every announcement of layoffs that appeared in the *Wall Street Journal* for companies quoted on the New York Stock Exchange for the 28 years between 1970 and 1997. There were 3,878 such announcements, concerning 1,176 companies. The findings of Farber and Hallock are unambiguous: on average, share prices *fall* in the wake of a layoff announcement. The fall in the share price subsequent to a layoff is admittedly weak, on the order of 0.4 percent, but it is indeed a fall and not a rise, as the theory of stock-market-driven layoffs would predict. All the other studies of the problem come to the same conclu-sion, both as regards the direction of the price movement—a fall instead of a rise—and its narrow spread—the average fall is never more than 1 percent. These results do not signify that the share price of a particular firm never rises after it cuts jobs. They simply signify that to elevate the example of Michelin, or some other large company whose share price did go higher in the wake of a mass layoff, to the status of an "economic law" runs counter to the facts of the matter. In economics, as in other domains, laws are only formulated on the basis of a very large number of observations, and they express general tendencies that evidently do not exclude a certain amount of variation. In the case at hand, if there is a law, it goes against the notion of stock-market-driven layoffs: *on average, the share price of a firm that cuts jobs falls.* This finding means simply that firms that resort to mass layoffs have, on average, a worse profit outlook than other firms. For that matter, a recent article by Sherrilyn Billger and Kevin Hallock finds that CEOs who are responsible for mass layoffs have higher chances of being fired themselves.[21]

The market and inequality

The destruction of jobs, which we see occurring in all industrialized countries, is thus not the fruit of a totally deregulated financial capitalism profiting exclusively from globalization. Certainly there do exist job destructions linked to international commerce and flows of speculative capital, but their extent is very limited compared to the amount of restructuring of the apparatus of production caused by changes in demand and technological innovation. We cannot overemphasize that this process, which creates and destroys millions of jobs every year, has an essential result: the growth of productivity. It is this growth that allows the majority of citizens to dispose of more and more goods and services. This unceasing process of job creation and destruction forms the primary matrix of the market economies grounded in the private ownership of the means of production (what is commonly called "capitalism"). In this regard, developments in the countries of the former Communist bloc are striking. Estonia, for example, liberalized its economy with brutal swiftness, beginning at the end of 1990. Using survey data on the movements of jobs and manpower since 1989, John Haltiwanger and Milan Vodopivec have found that the transition to a market economy was accompanied by a rapid rise in job destruction and creation. Job creation was practically null in 1989, when Estonia was still living in the era of central planning. In 1995 liberalization had largely been accomplished, and rates of job destruction and creation were of the same order as in the United States or in France.[22] Research on the shift from the planned economy of the former Soviet Union to the market economy of the Russia of today reaches a similar conclusion. In the former Soviet Union, there were few job reallocations and productivity growth was very weak. Since 1992, when firms had to start adapting more or less rapidly to the functioning of a market economy, the number of job reallocations has progressively risen, becoming comparable to those observed in western Europe from 1996 on. As well, the growth of productivity spiked upward after 1996, and is very strongly correlated to the reallocation of jobs.[23]

The market economy and the centrally planned economy are totally different with respect to the process of job destruction and creation, since they are grounded in two opposing logics. A planned economy is directed by the choices of the public authorities; a market economy is directed by private interests, especially by profit. The quest for profit is what drives the perpetual movement of innovation. Innovations lead to new products, new firms, and new industries, and cause procedures that had prevailed in the past to vanish. In the last analysis, it is the search for profit that is the motor of growth.[24] An economy of free markets is perpetually agitated by the attempts of firms to appropriate new business opportunities; some of these attempts are successful—temporarily, for the competition never rests—and others fail. A market economy is a seething ebullition of trials and errors, successes and setbacks, creations and destructions. By its very nature, this ebullition is unpredictable, and that is why it does not exist (on the same scale, at any rate) in a planned economy. A market economy is characterized by *permanent* and, above all, *inevitable* uncertainty, inseparable from the competition in which entrepreneurs engage in their hunt for profit. This unpredictable character of the market economy makes it intolerable to many, if not the majority. It is difficult to take on board the fact that the increase of wealth is inseparable from the radical uncertainty that the market economy engenders. Although uninterrupted progress without uncertainty about tomorrow would be preferable, the market economy is not capable of offering both these dishes on the same menu.[25]

There is another major flaw in the way market economies function: their efficiency is indissolubly linked to an unequal division of wealth.[26]

The permanent flux of job destruction and creation produces gains for the collectivity as a whole, but they are not automatically shared out according to the merits and responsibilities of each individual. The worker in a traditional textile factory who loses her job due to competition from low-wage countries is not to blame for her situation. The department head at Marks and Spencer who sees the store in which he works close its doors is not responsible for the changing tastes of consumers. The process of creative destruction *inevitably* produces this type of random outcome. The industrialization of western countries took place under conditions of atrocious suffering.[27] Even today millions of persons derive little benefit from economic growth in the richest countries. Intrinsically the market remains a formidable machine for creating wealth, but also for causing exclusion. These two phenomena are inseparable; in spurring the hunt for profit, the market enriches some but impoverishes others, often those who are already the poorest to start with.

Liberty, efficiency, equality

Does the efficiency of market economies in creating wealth suffice to compensate for the parallel production of inequality, and individual and global uncertainty? Some think so; others judge this cohabitation of wealth, inequality, and uncertainty to be indecent. Heightened awareness of the failings of the market gave rise to methods of organizing society that denied private property and free exchange, replacing them with the collectivization of the means of production and with central planning. Recent history instructs us, though, that the complete rejection of the market can lead to catastrophic situations. Systems of production grounded in the central planning of production proved to be incapable of reconciling respect for individual liberty with efficiency and equity.

The failure of the systems that reject the market altogether yields valuable lessons on certain of its virtues, which too often tend to be overlooked. Amartya Sen, the Nobel prize winner for economics in 1998, highlights this when he states that "the focus in assessing the market mechanism has tended to be on the *results* it ultimately generates, such as the incomes or the utilities yielded by the markets. This is not a negligible issue. . . . But the more immediate case for the freedom of market transaction lies in the basic importance of that freedom itself. We have good reasons to buy and sell, to exchange, and to seek lives that can flourish on the basis of transactions. To deny that freedom in general would be in itself a major failing of a society. This fundamental recognition is *prior* to any theorem we may or may not be able to prove . . . in showing what the culmination outcomes of markets are in terms of incomes, utilities, and so on."[28] Sen reminds us that the first of the goods produced by the market economy is the exercise of freedom to exchange goods, including the fruits of one's own labor. Recognition of this virtue is not a novelty. We find it in thinkers as diverse as Adam Smith, Alexis de Tocqueville, Karl Marx,[29] and a whole lineage of socialists.[30] It leads to the acceptance, and even to the defense when necessary, of the market as a system for organizing economic life—what we in Europe call liberalism.

Recognition of the virtues of the market need not automatically lead to a cartoonish and vacuously optimistic version of liberalism, resting on the zealous defense of market freedom and private property and the rejection of any form of public regulation. "Naive" liberal thinking of this kind ignores all the knowledge acquired on the benefits and short-comings of the market. Our task is to elaborate institutions that will lead individuals, in exercising their free will, to make efficient and equitable decisions. The principle of the exercise of free will dictates that reforms should be conceived in the knowledge that every actor in economic life will take her decisions in accordance with the motives that are proper to her—in general, her own self-interest and the interest of those closest to her. So it is a matter of knowing as precisely as possible how behavior changes when the environment and institutions evolve. Such is the goal of the science of economics, which has made a great deal of progress in this area during the last twenty years. It is on the basis of this exploration of "real liberalism" that we hope to convince readers that it is possible to improve employment, manage uncertainty, and reduce inequality, while continuing to respect the free will of each individual.[31]

2

Work Cannot Be Parceled Out

In 1962, around 400,000 French men and women of working age were repatriated from Algeria. Alfred Sauvy, a specialist in demographic issues, recalled the anxiety that gripped certain members of the nation's Commission of Accounts at that time. One of them had observed that the number of jobs officially available amounted to scarcely 35,000, and had concluded that the number of unemployed persons in France would inevitably be increased by the difference, rising by 365,000.[1] In the months and years that followed, nothing occurred to validate these dark forebodings.

The destiny of the French people repatriated from Algeria illustrates one of the principal lessons of economic analysis, which recent research, with the help of survey data coming from many parts of the world, has only confirmed: in a sufficiently reactive society, there is no reason that an increase in the quantity of manpower available should increase the number of the unemployed. Curiously, those who recognize the soundness of this precept sometimes have difficulty in admitting that the converse is also true: there is no reason that a decrease in the quantity of manpower available should lower the number of the unemployed in the long run. Hence certain observers, well-informed ones at that, foresee that continental European countries which currently face high unemployment rates will return to full employment, and might even have to face a shortage of manpower, in the next ten years, because of the retirement of the baby boomers: soon there won't even be enough workers to fill the jobs on offer![2]

The idea that any country's economy, and a fortiori the world economy, contains a fixed number of jobs or hours of work that can be parceled out in different ways is false. When used to justify policies that reduce the length of the individual work week, it may lead to unintended consequences. It is, moreover, harmful when used to justify the withdrawal of mothers with children from the working population (thanks, for example, to parental education allowances). It can even be dangerous, as when it leads to the notion that getting rid of "superfluous" manpower (the Jews of Nazi Germany in the past, immigrants from many countries in the present) will give work back to indigenous residents.

The second half of the twentieth century saw many waves of migration caused by harsh political events. These large-scale population movements, difficult to predict, enable us to make precise observations of the impact of a sudden, massive influx of manpower. Such movements of manpower can actually be interpreted as natural experiments, with the planet as the laboratory in which the investigator observes the effects of sudden displacements of population. These various experiments teach us something important: in a sufficiently reactive economy, variations in the size of the population, no matter how sudden or large, have no more than a small impact on unemployment and wages.

The Mariel boatlift

On 4 April 1980, following a conflict with the Peruvian government, Fidel Castro ordered the guards posted in front of the Peruvian embassy in Havana withdrawn. Seizing the chance offered by this absence, almost 11,000 Cubans stormed into the embassy and demanded political asylum. Images were immediately broadcast worldwide of a multitude of hungry and thirsty men, women, and children who were even perched in trees and on the roof of the embassy. After difficult negotiations and under strong pressure from the international community, the Cuban government agreed to let all the asylum seekers in the embassy leave the country. They were taken in by Costa Rica, Spain, Peru, and the United States. To counter the negative image created by this event, Fidel Castro announced, in a speech of 20 April 1980 that remains famous,[3] that he was throwing open the port of Mariel so that anyone who wanted to quit the island of Cuba could do so. A veritable human tidal wave followed this speech: almost 90,000 Cubans left their country for the United

States in May alone.[4] It is estimated that by the time the port of Mariel was closed again in September 1980, more than 125,000 Cubans had emigrated. Half of them settled in Miami, causing the labor force there to rise by 7 percent. Scaled up to the size of a country like France, that figure would have meant that the labor force would suddenly have expanded by almost 2 million persons. Faced with such a demographic shock, certain observers would surely have predicted that France would soon have 2 million more unemployed on its hands than it had had previously. The upshot of the adventure of the Cuban refugees suggests that they would undoubtedly have been wrong.

Between April and July 1980, the unemployment rate soared in Miami, going from 5 percent to 7.1 percent. This sudden increase in unemployment aroused the kind of reaction one could predict. In some quarters the Cuban refugees were precipitately accused of taking work away from the least qualified Americans and causing rising insecurity.[5] At first sight, these figures would appear to prove that those are right who think that the number of jobs is bounded by (mysterious) limits that, in any case, do not depend on the size of the labor force. If they are, then expanding the labor force could do nothing except expand the volume of unemployment. One way to test this thesis—the only way, actually—is to address this question: what would have happened in Miami if the Mariel boatlift had never taken place?

An American economist, David Card, took on this problem.[6] But he is not a clairvoyant, just a professor at the University of California at Berkeley, incapable of knowing any better than anyone else what would have happened in Miami if the Mariel boatlift had not occurred. Economists very often encounter problems of this type. They try to solve them by comparing the real circumstance to a control situation, one that mirrors the real circumstance as closely as possible *without* the "disturbance" the effects of which they want to assess. In the case at hand, the Mariel boatlift constitutes the disturbance. Card had the idea of taking as his controls U.S. cities with economic and demographic profiles similar to those of Miami, but which had not been affected by the great wave of Cuban immigration in 1980. He picked Atlanta, Los Angeles, Houston, and Tampa-St. Petersburg. Like Miami, these four cities included large black and Hispanic communities, and had undergone similar changes in employment and unemployment in the years before the Mariel boatlift. Card compared the average movements of wages and unemployment in the black, Hispanic, and white communities in these five cities, taking into account differences of education, experience, marital status, industry sector, and amount of part-time work. His main findings as regards changes in unemployment are given in table 2.1.[7]

In 1979, a year before the Mariel boatlift, the unemployment rate in the white population of Miami reached 5.1 percent; in 1981, a year after the boatlift, it fell to 3.9 percent. In other words, the unemployment rate in the white population of Miami went down by 1.2 percentage points between 1979 and 1981. Over the same period, the unemployment rate in the white population of the control cities also went down, but only by 0.1 percentage points. The comparison between these two figures, 1.2 and 0.1, warrants the conclusion that the influx into Miami of Cuban manpower did not have a negative effect on employment within the white population. Neither did it have a negative effect on the black population, though that was the group most exposed to competition from the new refugees. It is true that the unemployment rate in the black population rose by 1.3 percentage points between 1979 and 1981, but in the same period it rose by 2.3 percentage points in the control cities. More generally, David Card's study shows that changes in the labor

Table 2.1
Unemployment Rates before and after the Mariel Boatlift

	Before Mariel 1979	After Mariel 1981	After-before difference
Whites			
Miami	5.1%	3.9%	−1.2
Control cities	4.4%	4.3%	−0.1
Blacks			
Miami	8.3%	9.6%	1.3
Control cities	10.3%	12.6%	2.3

Source: David Card, "The Impact of the Mariel Boatlift on the Miami Labor Market," table 6.

market in Miami and the control cities were very similar, well after the Mariel boatlift. Thus, the Cuban immigration had no significant effect on the wages and employment of persons living in Miami. After a very strong upsurge of unemployment immediately following the arrival of the new immigrants (remember that the unemployment rate in Miami went from 5 percent to 7.1 percent between April and May 1980), all data point to the fact that this city absorbed an exceptional influx of newcomers in the space of a year.

One objection quickly comes to mind. Might these results not be due to the flight of a large proportion of the resident population, which left to seek other jobs somewhere else because of the incoming tide of Cubans? Card was able to establish that, in the years following the massive upswing of the population of Miami in 1980, employment opportunities in this city did not degrade appreciably in comparison to the control cities. Thus, if there was a flight of the resident population, it was a small one at best. The majority of studies focusing on the United States, and on many other countries, come to analogous conclusions: the influx of migrants has a very weak impact on wages, employment, and the mobility of residents.[8] These results may occasion surprise, but they cannot be dodged. Let us see how economic analysis goes about explaining them.

Population and unemployment: Is there a link?

A fairly simple line of reasoning allows us to understand David Card's findings. It posits that each worker is remunerated—or remunerates himself if he is independent—in proportion to his capacity to produce wealth; or in other words, in proportion to his productivity. Let us suppose that productivity depends on his personal characteristics (educational level, professional experience, age, motivation, intelligence, etc.) *and* the means placed at his disposal (machines, offices, computers, transportation and communications infrastructure, health care system, etc.).[9] Let us agree to call the ensemble of these means "capital," and let us suppose that, when a new immigrant arrives, the economic system is sufficiently reactive to make the capital necessary for the exploitation of the productive faculties of this newcomer available very quickly.[10] Given these premises, the employment of established residents is not affected; there is simply one more person at work, in this case the new immigrant. On the other hand, his remuneration cannot exceed his productivity; otherwise he would never have been hired. It follows from this that the national wealth available to be shared by residents has not diminished. Indeed, it has grown by the difference between the productivity and the wage of the newcomer (equal to zero in the worst case). So the residents have at least as big a "pie" to share as before the arrival of the new immigrant, and their income has no reason to shrink. This simple line of reasoning makes it possible to state an essential result: if the capital necessary for the productive capacities of new immigrants to be exploited can be made available very rapidly, their arrival has no influence on either the employment or the wages of the people already there. This result applies to all situations in which the size of the labor force can vary, whether through immigration or, for that matter, through the lowering or raising of the age of retirement.

In reality, capital does not adapt instantaneously. A certain amount of time is needed for the means of production and the infrastructure to adapt to a large and unexpected influx of manpower. An increase in the labor force, which entails less capital per head, can then lead to a diminution in the productivity of residents. This fall in productivity itself entails a lowering of wages or, if wages are blocked from falling, unemployment. The ability certain countries have to rapidly adapt their means of production and their infrastructures is thus the key to the economic integration of immigrants. From this perspective, the results obtained by Card and by numerous studies on migration in the United States suggest that the adaptive capacity of capital is so strong in that country that the arrival of new immigrants has little or no influence on the wages and employment of residents. In the case of the Mariel boatlift, investment quickly flowed into the textile sector, which is very dynamic locally and which quickly absorbed a large portion of the Cuban manpower. Textiles had taken root and grown in Miami in the 1970s, in the wake of substantial population movements. Hence the massive immigration of 1980 occurred in a place where the dominant industry possessed know-how and resources allowing it to invest so as to quickly absorb large quantities of extra manpower. The slight impact of the Mariel boatlift is linked to this rapid mobilization of the capital necessary to put the influx of newcomers to work. Absent this capacity to quickly mobilize the necessary capital, the absorption of the new immigrants would have taken longer and the swelling of the labor force would have led to a fall in the productivity of residents over the entire period required for the stock of capital to adapt. Such a reduction of productivity must entail a lowering of wages if wages are flexible, or outright job destruction and unemployment if wages cannot fall. Thus, the higher the adaptive capacity of capital, the more transient the impact of the arrival of new immigrants on the employment and wages of residents. This condition obtains in the United States, but in countries where it does not, a migratory inflow will cause the wages and employment of residents to be depressed until the necessary capital has been mobilized.

Immigration in Europe

The Évian accords proclaiming the independence of Algeria were signed in March 1962 and approved by referendum in April of that year. Thereafter, almost 900,000 people were repatriated back to France in 1962 alone, the vast majority of whom chose to settle in departments (departments are the basic territorial and administrative units in France) in the southern part of the country. At the start of this chapter we recalled the nightmarish predictions which this exceptional migratory wave provoked. In point of fact, the French economy absorbed it fairly quickly and without great harm to workers in metropolitan centers.

Jennifer Hunt, a professor at the University of Montreal, has assessed the impact of the 1962 immigration on persons residing in metropolitan centers.[11] To do so, she compared the pattern of unemployment and wages in the 90 metropolitan departments of France between 1962 and 1967, when those repatriated from Algeria represented 1.6 percent of the workforce. This research project was made challenging by the great diversity of economic activities and socio-professional categories from one department to another. Among the various factors capable of influencing employment, Hunt strove to isolate those that could be directly attributed to the stimulus of the workers repatriated from Algeria in

1962. She was able to show that the departments that took in the most returnees had rates of unemployment not very different from the other departments. She calculates that the arrival of ten repatriated workers in 1962 led, by 1967, to two extra unemployed persons among the residents; and also that the average wage was at most 1.3 percent lower in 1967 than what it would have been in the same year if the returnees had stayed in Algeria.

The impact of the Algerian returnees on the wages and employment of residents in metropolitan centers was thus limited, but still greater than that observed in the United States after the Mariel boatlift. If we rely on Hunt's figures, an influx of returnees proportionally as large for France as the Mariel boatlift was for the city of Miami would have entailed a reduction of 5.7 percent in wages and an increase in the unemployment rate among residents of 1.4 percentage points between 1962 and 1967, which is far from negligible. The North American labor market indisputably has a greater capacity to absorb manpower than the French labor market does. Changes in the American population of working age during the 1990s supply a striking illustration of this difference.[12] This population grew by more than 10 percent between 1990 and 2000. By the end of the decade, the American unemployment rate was 4.5 percent, an extremely low rate, illustrating that the United States was able to absorb a large number of new entrants onto the labor market in a very short time. The situation in France is very different: the working-age population grew by a much smaller 3.8 percent between 1990 and 2000, yet at the end of this period, the unemployment rate was twice as high in France as it was in the United States. Quite evidently, it was not some particularly large flow of entrants onto the labor market that helped to keep the unemployment rate higher in France than in the United States during the recent past.

The conflicts in Bosnia and Kosovo during the 1990s also triggered a sizeable wave of immigration in the direction of many European countries. For example, between 1994 and 1997 in Switzerland, persons from the former Yugoslavia formed the largest subgroup among workers born outside the European Union. In Sweden they are the largest immigrant nationality after Finns, and Austria took in 100,000 Bosnian refugees between 1992 and 1995. The economists Joshua Angrist of

Massachusetts Institute of Technology and Adriana Kugler of the Pompeu Fabra University of Barcelona grasped the opportunity of this sudden and substantial influx of immigrants to study the effects of an increase in the foreign-born workforce on the different receiving countries.[13] They collected and analyzed data on population movements in eighteen European countries. They find that on average an increase of 10 percent in the foreign-born part of the labor force leads to a fall in employment among residents of between 0.2 and 0.7 percentage points. Once again, it is apparent that the impact of immigration on employment among residents is limited in overall terms. But their study does not stop with this average estimate. They were also able to show that the impact of immigration is not the same in all receiving countries and that it depends, in particular, on the legislation governing layoff procedures on barriers to entry onto the markets for goods. The higher the cost of laying workers off and the higher the barriers to entry onto the markets for goods, the greater the negative impact of immigration on employment among residents.

Analysis of the impact of migrations on the labor market formally contradicts the notion that the number of jobs is a given, independent of the size of the population of working age. In fact, the diametrically opposite formulation comes closer to capturing reality: the number of jobs rises and falls to match, more or less quickly, the number of persons who want to work. This is not an astonishing revelation in light of the description of the way the labor market functions given in the previous chapter, where we saw that employment is the outcome of an ongoing and massive recomposition of the apparatus of production. In a setting in which millions of jobs are created and destroyed every year, it would be surprising if the number of jobs were an intangible given, independent of shifts in the population.

An end of unemployment, or more unemployment, in the near to mid term?

In many OECD countries, expected demographic developments will lead to significant declines in the growth (and sometimes the levels) of the working-age population over the next decades.[14] The lessons we derived from an examination of migratory movements shed light on the consequences of such a prospect: there is no reason to expect reduced unemployment to follow from the diminution of the working-age population. Since this diminution is expected to be slow and steady, there is little chance that the reduction in the number of new entrants onto the labor market will lead to a reduction, even a transitory one, of unemployment.

On this front, we should therefore not expect a fundamental shift that will improve the performance of the labor market. Quite the contrary, the demographic trends we face are likely to increase social transfer payments and so risk hindering employment. For the shrinkage of the labor force actually has the corollary of an increase in the number of retirees per head of the working-age population: on average, this ratio increased moderately, from 23 percent to 26 percent during the 1990s, for the OECD countries, but demographic projections indicate that a sharp increase to 42 percent is projected until 2025. The numbers of retirees per head of the working-age population are set to reach high levels in 2025 in many European and, in particular, central European countries. In contrast, they will remain moderate in Mexico, Iceland, Turkey, Ireland, Portugal, and the United States.[15] Such a phenomenal change results from a twofold shift: the retirement of the baby boomers born in the 1950s and 1960s, and increased life expectancy, which automatically lengthens the period of retirement. This rise in the number of retirees per person of working age implies that the cost of retirements as a portion of GDP is going to rise steadily in many OECD countries, assuming we wish to guarantee replacement rates equivalent to those that obtain today. Thus, we will need to find a way to allocate extra percentage points of GDP to retirements between now and 2040. This can be done either by increasing pension contributions or by extending the length of time over which they are paid in. In order to underwrite completely the missing percentage points of GDP, it would be necessary to make all wage-earners contribute for many extra years in the most aging OECD countries—a scenario that is hard to envisage. Consequently, in these countries, the social security contributions necessary to cover the cost of retirements will have to be increased, and that will risk increasing the cost of labor and may prove detrimental to employment, notably the employment of those with few skills, which is the kind most vulnerable to increased labor costs. In sum, the diminution of the working-age population, far from leading to a hypothetical return to full employment, will have an opposite tendency to magnify the problems facing the labor market.

The shortened work week and employment

Before the French Revolution, workers' corporations imposed rules specifying long periods during which waged work was forbidden: workers did not show up on Sundays, or on Mondays following payday; took numerous breaks during the working day; worked a reduced schedule at harvest time; and were mostly adults, since child labor was restricted. As a result there were 164 nonworking days a year in France in the seventeenth century. The Allarde and Le Chapelier laws, passed in 1791, abolished the workers' corporations and allowed employers to set the amount of time worked. The amount of time employees spent at work therefore rose considerably, reaching 4,500 hours per year at the beginning of the nineteenth century, whereas two hundred years before, agricultural laborers had worked between 1,800 and 2,000 hours per year.[16] In this context, the reduction of the time spent at work became the focus of recurrent social conflict. Progress on this front was slow, and was sometimes even halted or reversed. For example, the weekly day of rest introduced by law in 1814 was legally abolished in 1880. Its numerous opponents were concerned about the bad effects of free time on workers, the loss of production, and the closure of pastry shops on Sundays.[17] Only in 1906 was the weekly day of rest established on a firm footing. The 8-hour day and the 48-hour week were prescribed (albeit with plenty of loopholes) in 1919, while the 40-hour week and two weeks of yearly paid vacation date from 1936. The third, fourth, and fifth weeks of paid vacation were added in 1956, 1963, and 1982. The legal work week went to 39 hours in 1982 and finally to 35 hours in 2000 for firms with more than 20 employees (and in 2002 for those with fewer than 20 employees).

Historically, the main goal of the drive to reduce the amount of time spent at work was to improve the lives of laborers. Sometimes it was part of a militant struggle to organize society on a different basis altogether, in which work would no longer hold a preponderant place. But by the end of the 1970s, with rising mass unemployment in some countries of continental Europe, the essential reason for reducing the length of time individuals spent at work became that of parceling work out more widely in order to bring down the rate of unemployment. The French prime ministers Pierre Mauroy and Lionel Jospin used this argument explicitly when they shortened the work week by law in 1982 and 2000. In announcing his employment program on 15 September 1981, Pierre Mauroy declared roundly that "the reduction of the work week constitutes by far the most effective measure against unemployment."[18] And Martine Aubry, the architect of the 35-hour law brought in by the government of Lionel Jospin, disclosed in an interview published in the newspaper *Le Monde* on 8 October 2003 that the principal objective of the 35-hour week "was to get the maximum number of persons into a job." This is not a view taken exclusively by left-of-center governments, for the so-called Robien law passed in June 1996 under the right-wing government of Alain Juppé also had the goal of giving firms an incentive to hire by reorganizing and reducing working time on a negotiated basis.

At first sight, the notion that reducing individual working time is a way to share employment more widely seems to be self-evident: in a world in which the production of firms was an intangible given, a fixed number of hours of work would be needed to achieve this amount of production, and if everyone worked less, firms would have to hire more employees in order to meet their orders. But that is not the world we live in.[19] The economic environment is always highly uncertain, and a massive number of jobs is constantly being redeployed within firms. Some of them do indeed have orders to meet within a few weeks or a few months, and can therefore be incentivized to hire extra personnel. But these hires will be temporary, because what determines the survival and growth of firms is the capacity to keep the customers they have and to win new ones. In the last analysis, the impact of the reduction of individual working time on employment depends on how it affects the competitiveness of firms. Government authorities have been aware of this fact for some time, for the Aubry laws, and the Robien law before them, provide for substantial "assistance." The Aubry laws reduce the payroll charges on firms that reduce their employees' working time; these lowered payroll costs currently amount to 0.7 percent of GDP, or twice the budget of the RMI, the income support program that provides basic welfare.[20]

It remains to be seen whether shorter working hours enhance competitiveness. They will do so if they give firms the incentive to organize themselves better, and if they impel wage-earners to work more efficiently, without raising the cost of manpower too much. For the supporters of the 35-hour week, this was the most likely outcome,[21] but only empirical studies have the capacity to tell us whether reality has unfolded according to this scenario. Unfortunately, few studies thus far have evaluated the impact of reduced working time using survey data that bear on large numbers of firms, or that follow the paths of large numbers of persons in the labor market.[22] Jennifer Hunt has analyzed the consequences of reductions in the length of the working week negotiated sector by sector in Germany between 1984 and 1994.[23] Each sector was able to negotiate a different legal or "standard" work week. In industry, for example, the average standard work week has gone from 40 hours in 1984 to 38.8 hours in 1988 and 37.7 hours in 1994. The explicit aim of many of these negotiated reductions in the standard work week was to increase employment by sharing the work more widely. The variability in the length of the standard work week in different sectors constitutes a precious mine of information for evaluating how measures that reduce the legal work week affect hours actually worked, wages, and employment. Hunt was able to demonstrate that hours actually worked did decrease in step with the standard work week. On the other hand, she finds that the level of employment was not affected by changes to the standard work week, and that monthly wages held steady. The German experiment in the sharing of work thus allowed those who kept their jobs to benefit from shorter hours without loss of income, but did not contribute to bringing down unemployment.

Bruno Crépon and Francis Kramarz, who belong to the research unit of INSEE (the French National Institute for Statistics and Economic

Studies), have examined the effects of the law of 1 February 1982 that lowered the legal work week from 40 to 39 hours while leaving wages unchanged.[24] They find that workers who actually benefited from the reduction of the work week between 1981 and 1982 lost their jobs *more frequently* than those whose work week was already less than 39 hours in 1981. To be precise, they estimate that 6.2 percent of wage-earners working 40 hours in 1981 had lost their jobs in 1982, whereas only 3.2 percent of those who were already working 39 hours or less in 1981 no longer had jobs in 1982. They were careful to make sure that the individual qualities of workers were not the true causes of this difference in the frequency of job loss, and thus conclude that the change to 39 hours had no positive impact on employment, even in the short term.

Evaluating the shift down to 35 hours is much trickier, since the Aubry laws contained a complex mix of reductions in work time, financial assistance, and flexibility in scheduling. The often-quoted figure of 350,000 jobs created (at a minimum) by these laws has no solid foundation. And even if it does turn out to be correct, that is not enough to prove that the reduction in working time did have a beneficial effect on employment. We cannot rule out the possibility that the Aubry laws would have favored employment even more if they had consisted of diminished payroll charges *without* a shorter work week. After all, the two studies summarized above, which analyze the reduction of the work week in isolation from all other factors, do not demonstrate that this measure had any positive effect on employment, and we will see in the next chapter that programs to alleviate payroll charges actually do seem to have made it possible to create many jobs. These results give us no reason to believe that the section of the Aubry laws that brought individual working time down was a job creator. But at present we lack rigorous comparative evaluations of the kind done, for example, to assess the effects of the Mariel boatlift, and while we await them (assuming they will someday be carried out), prudent reserve is de rigueur.

The belief that reducing the amount of time spent at work by each individual systematically creates more jobs, just like the suspicion that immigrants take jobs away from citizens of the destination countries, springs from a mistaken notion of how the labor market works: the belief that there exists a quantity of jobs or hours of work dictated by some transcendent force. This notion is diametrically opposed to reality. Jobs are fragile things. They can bloom and wither very quickly and in very large numbers. Their existence depends on certain characteristics of the economic environment, on which the government can act, and which will be examined in the following chapters.

3

Wages Are Not (Always) the Enemy of Employment

It is 17 February 1995. Jacques Chirac is delivering a speech to launch his campaign for the presidency of France. He alludes to the risk of social breakdown, and then makes this statement:

Some have gone so far as to assert, echoing the plan commission charged with guiding us toward the frontier of the year 2000, that there will be no upturn, no return to growth, without a freeze or limit on the purchasing power of wage-earners. Look at this, they are proposing to reinvent the incomes policy of the 1960s, which directed the employees' and employers' unions to arbitrate, at the top, between wages and employment. As though the pay slip were the enemy of employment. As though a franc paid in wages were a franc lost to the economy, a franc that doesn't consume, a franc that doesn't save, a useless franc. Some are even prepared to contest the principle of the minimum wage, which according to them has perverse effects on employment. I can only say that such discourses leave me quite uneasy.[1]

Do we detect a "Keynesian" stance in this utterance by the future head of state, challenging the "liberalism" (in the European sense of the term) of the supporters of Édouard Balladur, one of his competitors? We know that for followers of Keynes, high wages guarantee strong consumption by households, which gives businesses an incentive to hire in order to meet this consumer demand. Conversely, for "liberal" free-marketeers, wage rises destroy jobs because they undercut the profitability of firms. Who is right? A priori, they both are, because it is always possible to support either view by adducing a coherent theoretical model and a few well-chosen historical examples. In recent years economists have made an effort to decide this question with the help of statistical resources and methods of crunching the data which their predecessors did not possess. Today we can still say that both sides are right, but now we have a somewhat clearer idea of the conditions under which each is right.

A tale of fast food

On 1 April 1992 the minimum wage rose drastically in the state of New Jersey, by almost 19 percent. However, it stayed where it was in the neighboring state of Pennsylvania. David Card and Alan Krueger, then both professors of economics at Princeton University, took advantage of this "natural" experiment to try to assess the effects of a rise in the minimum wage on the hiring of those to whom the minimum wage applied. To do so, they compared changes in the level of employment in fast-food restaurants situated in New Jersey and Pennsylvania.[2] Fast-food places for the most part employ manpower with few skills at low wages, most often at the minimum wage. Hence, their profitability depends directly on where this wage is set, and one would expect employment in this sector to be particularly sensitive to variations in it. According to Card and Krueger, more than 90 percent of the professional economists in the United States at that time defended an elementary line of reasoning leading to a diagnosis from which there was no appeal: a rise in the minimum wage would reduce the profitability of the fast-food restaurant sector in New Jersey and would thus destroy fast-food jobs there. Since the minimum wage had not changed in Pennsylvania, one ought to expect a much better employment picture in fast-food places in Pennsylvania than in New Jersey.

In order to test this diagnosis, Card and Krueger collected data on 473 restaurants in the fast-food sector. An initial survey was done in February and March 1992, before the rise in the minimum wage came into effect. A second survey followed in November and December 1992, about eight months after the minimum wage was boosted. The authors state the conclusion yielded by their analysis of the data from these two surveys in forthright language: the rise in the minimum wage had no negative impact on employment in New Jersey fast-food places. It might even have had a slightly positive impact. This result appeared topsy-turvy to many economists, and reaction followed swiftly.

In the first place, doubts were raised about the quality of the data provided by the surveys, which had been carried out by telephone and were therefore alleged to have yielded information less reliable than the compulsory declarations the same employers had to make to the fiscal authorities. Analysis of data from this latter source did cast doubt initially on the validity of the study's conclusions, but Card and Krueger finally succeeded in proving that their results were not fundamentally altered by the use of data from fiscal statements.[3] Another objection put to them was that they had neglected the consequences of a rise in the minimum wage on the *number* of restaurants in business. It cannot be excluded that the higher wage did put a brake on the opening of new establishments. In order to meet this objection, Card and Krueger expanded their inquiry beyond employees in fast-food places alone, and evaluated the impact of the minimum wage on all young people aged 16 to 24. Their finding was that, relative to the whole United States, employment in this segment of the population in New Jersey had risen after that state raised its minimum wage. There is thus little likelihood that this rise put a damper on the opening of places employing a high percentage of young people.

Finally, criticism was aimed at the very principle of the research project, which was to assess the impact of the minimum wage by comparing changes in employment in a state where it had risen with those in another state that had not experienced such a rise. Many different factors could cause patterns of employment to diverge from one state to another, and this method does not eliminate their possible influence. The same vulnerability exists in medicine, which also tests new therapies in varied settings; medical researchers meet it by multiplying the number of experiments, so that the risk of wrongly attributing favorable changes in patients to a new therapy is limited. Card and Krueger applied the same principle by replicating their study in other cases in which the minimum wage had varied in the United States. They analyzed the consequences of the 27 percent increase in the minimum wage in California in 1988, which they estimate to have had no negative impact either on total employment, or on that of young people, or on the employment of wage-earners in the retail trade (the last two being the groups most affected by this wage level).[4] Their subsequent studies, following federal decisions of 1990 and 1991 that extended the 27 percent rise in the minimum wage to the whole of the United States, confirm these conclusions:[5] increases in the minimum wage occurring in the United States at the end of the 1980s and during the 1990s did not have a negative impact on employment.

Is it time, once and for all, to reject the dominant theory that every increase in the minimum wage, by undercutting the profitability of businesses, has a negative effect on employment? Not quite yet.

How does the minimum wage act on employment?

In reality, labor economists have known for a long time that the imposition of a minimum wage is capable of having a positive and lasting impact on employment. George Stigler, in a fundamental article published in 1946, had already explained why a rise in the minimum wage could increase the number of hires if "an employer has a significant degree of control over the wage rate he pays."[6] This slightly opaque sentence refers to the *degree of competition* prevailing on the labor market. Stigler had noted that economists were generally assuming that the labor market functions according to the rules of "perfect competition" when they pondered the effects of the minimum wage. In a situation of perfect competition, employers would engage in a fierce struggle to attract highly mobile manpower. This intense competition would induce them to set wages practically equivalent to the productivity of the workers they recruited, because they would fear that otherwise their workers would abandon them for competing employers. The gap between what a worker contributes (his productivity) and what he costs (his wage) would then be insignificant.[7] If, in this setting, the government imposes a minimum wage *higher* than the wage determined by the play of competition, certain workers will cost their firms more than they bring in. The firms will end up letting these workers go. So the (minimum) wage is indeed the enemy of employment.

But reality seldom resembles this situation of perfect competition. In particular, the incessant process of job creation and destruction that we detailed in chapter 1 obliges workers to spend time, energy, and resources to find a job, or to find a new one. When a worker receives a job offer and thinks about turning it down, he knows that he will probably have to spend considerable time and resources searching before he receives a fresh offer. We are a long way from the ideal world of perfect competition, in which every individual who refuses a job offer can instantaneously go and get hired somewhere else. The labor market is viscous, and this quality has the initial effect of diminishing the intensity of the struggle in which employers engage to attract manpower. In reality, every employer thus holds a *monopsony power*[8] from which she can benefit by setting a wage *lower* than the wage that perfect competition would have produced. The gap between productivity and the wage is no longer negligible; there is now a "margin" between what an employee costs and what he brings in to the firm.

If the state then decides to set the minimum wage very slightly above the wage chosen by the employer, the latter sees her margin appreciably reduced. The margin does remain positive, though, and so there is no reason for the employer to let the employee go. But there is more: the increase in the minimum wage will give some people who are out of work an incentive to look harder for a job, and to consider offers they had previously turned down. We will then observe *more* people wanting to work, in order to get the minimum wage set by the state, than there had been who were willing to accept the (lower) wage chosen by an employer exploiting her monopsony power. Since the employer is realizing a positive margin for each worker who is getting minimum wage, she has an interest in hiring more workers. The minimum wage is no longer the enemy of employment.

Alas, this sequence cannot be reiterated indefinitely. Each new increase in the minimum wage attracts new workers but reduces the margin of benefit on those already employed. If the state continues to increase the minimum wage, some workers will wind up costing more than they bring in, and they will then be let go. The minimum wage becomes the enemy of employment once again. This "noncompetitive" vision of the labor market, inspired by the ideas of George Stigler, is of interest because it lets us see that rises in the minimum wage do not always exert influence in the *same* direction. Everything depends on conditions at the outset. If the minimum wage is low, bordering on basic welfare, an increase in it attracts new workers whom firms have an interest in hiring. But if the minimum wage is high at the outset, every increase incentivizes firms to trim from their payrolls those employees whose productivity has been overtaken by the new level of the minimum wage, without hiring an equivalent number of new, more productive, workers.

Hence the minimum wage can be either helpful or harmful to employment. A cycling metaphor offers an apt summary of this debate: a labor market in which a minimum wage obtains is like a hill climb followed by a descent in the Tour de France. In the uphill stage, each extra pedal stroke brings you closer to the summit, where the level of employment is at its maximum, but in the downhill stage, each extra pedal stroke takes you farther away from it. Above all, it is a question of knowing if the pack of workers is still ascending the hill, or if it has already begun the descent. The story of the fast-food places in New Jersey would seem to indicate that in the United States the pack was still moving uphill. That is not necessarily the case everywhere else.

France versus the United States

For more than four decades, the minimum wage has moved very differently in France and in the United States. As figure 3.1 shows, in France the minimum wage has not stopped climbing since the start of the 1960s, while in the United States it is worth less in 2004 than it was in 1960! In France over this period, the purchasing power of an hour of work paid at the rate set by the minimum wage has multiplied by two and a half, while in the United States the purchasing power of an hour of work paid at the federal minimum wage has *diminished*. This diverging pattern, amplified by increases in payroll taxes in France, has led today to very different labor costs for low-skilled manpower. In France, the average cost of labor at minimum wage is about 100 percent higher than it is in the United States.[9] The gap is so great that we may legitimately ask whether the United States and France are both on the same side of the hill. The former, it would seem, is still pedaling uphill, where increases in the minimum wage can create jobs, whereas the latter finds

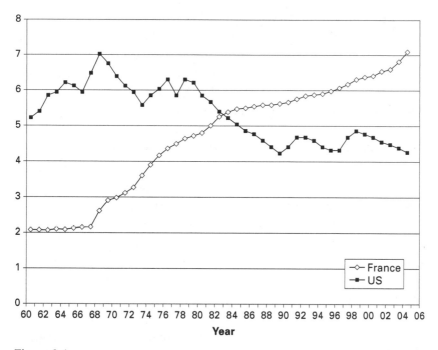

Figure 3.1
The minimum wage in France and the United States between 1960 and 2004.
Movement of the gross real minimum hourly wage in euros as of the year 2002,
assuming that €1 = $1.1. Source: Data from the International Labor Office.

itself on the downslope, where the same increases carry us further away
from the optimum.

A study conducted by a French-American team composed of John
Abowd, Francis Kramarz, David Margolis, and Thomas Philippon confirms this intuition using a simple but clever methodological procedure.[10]
Their method is based on the fact that, with each increase in the
minimum wage, there are workers whose wages are overtaken by this
increase, whereas the wages of workers who are making a little bit more
are not. Abowd and his colleagues had the idea of comparing the outcomes of workers who were "overtaken"—in other words, those whose
wages rose—with the outcomes of workers who were not overtaken—
those whose wage was not affected. This quasi-experimental method is

close to that utilized by David Card and Alan Krueger in their study of fast-food places in New Jersey. It consists of evaluating the performance of a test group affected by a measure (here, workers overtaken by the rise in the minimum wage) and that of a control group endowed with similar characteristics but unaffected by the measure in question (here, workers already making a little more than the new minimum wage, who are therefore not overtaken by it). In order to execute this strategy, data from samples covering several tens of thousands of persons between 1990 and 1998 were crunched. In the United States, the employment outlook of persons in the test group, the ones whose wage was overtaken by increases in the minimum wage, do not vary significantly from that of persons in the control group. In France, on the other hand, those belonging to the test group run a greater risk of losing their jobs than those in the control group. Increases in the minimum wage therefore appear to have little or no downside in the United States but appear to undermine employment in France.

These results nevertheless leave open an important aspect of the problem. George Stigler's argument for explaining the positive impact of the minimum wage on employment rests on a modification of the behavior of workers: the minimum wage can raise employment by increasing the number of persons wanting to be hired at minimum wage and therefore willing to make an effort to find a job. Thus it is possible that every rise in the minimum wage drives French firms to let some of their employees go, while at the same time facilitating the recruitment of other, supposedly more productive persons, and therefore promoting an increase in total employment in the end. If that were the case, one ought to observe increases in the minimum wage leading to a rise in entries into employment at the new wage levels. The study by Abowd and his colleagues invalidates this hypothetical result. Rather, it finds that a rise in the minimum wage has a negative impact on entries into employment in France. In sum, the study concludes that a rise in the minimum wage contributes not only to increased job destruction but also to diminished job creation. The finding is thus unambiguous: increases in the cost of labor to the higher levels set by the minimum wage lead to reductions in the employment of those with few skills in France. The United States and France are, indeed, not on the same side of the hill.[11]

Guaranteeing both wages and employment

The observation that the *cost* of labor exerts a negative impact on employment does not mean that *wages* should necessarily be lowered. In France there is a considerable gap between the cost of labor and wages, and it is perfectly possible to reduce the former without reducing the latter. On average, when an employer disburses €100, the worker receives a net wage of €55, before paying tax on the income. This difference between the cost of labor and the net wage comes from what are called "payroll taxes" or social security taxes—contributions to the state's coffers made by wage-earners and their employers that are used to finance public expenditure on health, retirement, and unemployment insurance. Policies to reduce payroll taxes put in place by governments of both the right and the left aimed to reduce the cost of labor without cutting back on the net wages received by employees. These policies brought the contributions paid by employers down from 45 percent to 25 percent for workers being paid the minimum wage, which entails that a labor cost of €100 guarantees a net wage of €69 at that level.

The effectiveness of these policies is not in doubt. The most complete and fully documented study was carried out by Bruno Crépon and Rosenn Desplatz.[12] Using a sample of 90,000 firms, they assessed the impact that payroll tax relief for employers, introduced in 1995 and 1996, has had on low wages by comparing the performance of firms that benefited from this relief against that of firms that did not so benefit. They estimate that this payroll tax relief for employers had created, or preserved, around 460,000 jobs at the end of 1997.[13] Their results, summarized in table 3.1, indicate that this relief created mainly unskilled jobs, but also skilled ones, both in the industry sector and the service sector. The rise in unskilled employment was foreseen, but that in skilled employment may cause surprise, since this kind of employment is unaffected by the lower payroll taxes. Two phenomena combine to explain the rise in skilled employment. For one thing, the hiring of low-skilled workers enhances the efficiency of skilled workers, who can delegate some of their tasks or benefit from having a larger number of helpers. For another, the reduction in the cost of low-skilled labor improves the overall profitability of firms benefiting from this payroll tax relief. Their

Table 3.1
Job creation due to payroll tax relief in France (in thousands)

	Industry	Services	Combined
Total employment	150	310	460
Skilled employment	70	150	220
Unskilled employment	80	160	240

Note: unskilled employment corresponds to unskilled workers and employees, apprentices, and interns.
Source: Bruno Crépon and Rosenn Desplatz, "Une nouvelle évaluation des effets des allègements de charges sociales sur les bas salaires."

competitiveness rises, they gain market share, and thus they recruit both unskilled and skilled workers.

The assessment of Crépon and Desplatz does not take into account the financing of the payroll tax relief. We cannot exclude a priori that the extra social security contributions necessary to cover its cost may ultimately impose a drag on job creation and nullify the benefit of the relief. This risk is low, for as table 3.1 shows, payroll tax relief on low wages creates a lot of employment. From that employment flow new receipts for the fisc, and savings on unemployment insurance and welfare payments. In the long run, the gains realized thanks to this job creation can thus compensate for the contributions required to underwrite the payroll tax relief.

Lowered payroll taxes and solidarity

If the cost of labor at the level of the minimum wage is still the enemy of employment, is that a reason to abolish the minimum wage? No, but it is a reason to reduce its cost to firms yet further. Payroll tax relief makes this reduction possible. Yet some people view this approach as no more than an excessively generous "handout" to the employers concerned. Such criticism neglects the fact that payroll taxes are always extracted from households in the end, whatever their form. While it is true that the households that own businesses are richer on average than others, and reduced payroll taxes on low wages might have a tendency to increase their incomes, this is not a reason to reject a policy that has the virtue of creating low-skilled jobs. It is possible, and can even be desirable, to limit the eventual increase in income of the most well-off households by means of greater progressivity in income tax. We shall return to this point in chapter 5.

There is a redistributive aspect to the policy of reducing payroll taxes that should also be mentioned. In its absence, the firms employing the largest number of minimum-wage earners—which are often small businesses active in markets where competition is keen—must bear *on their own* the *collective* decision to set the minimal standard for wages at a high level (or a decent level, if you prefer). It is moreover unjust that persons should be excluded from employment on account of this collective decision, which redounds to the profit of some but not that of others. For the minimum wage to be an instrument for the redistribution of resources to the benefit of the least-favored workers, its impact on the cost of labor must be held down. Otherwise, the minimum wage can have consequences quite opposite to those intended: it can increase inequality by preventing those least qualified from finding a job. Other forms of redistribution financed by all taxpayers are conceivable, like the negative income tax, for example. The choice of a high minimum wage assumes solidarity on the part of all taxpayers in order to be effective and equitable, and the way for that solidarity to be manifested is for payroll tax relief for businesses that employ manpower at minimum wage to be financed by society at large.

Alleviations in payroll taxes make it possible to hold down increases in the cost of labor at the minimum wage while preserving the purchasing power of this wage. But that is not enough. It is also necessary to create conditions in which paid work is financially more attractive than staying out of the job market. We shall see in the next chapter that these conditions do not always obtain.

4
Work Must Pay

Work at what price?

Before 15 July 1980, an employee who was the victim of a workplace accident in the state of Kentucky received a payment proportional to his or her wage during the entire period of convalescence. There was an upper limit on these payments of $131 per week. On 15 July 1980, the limit was raised to $217 per week, a rise of 66 percent, with the result that the best-paid wage-earners were substantially better compensated for workplace accidents that occurred after that date. This increase made a considerable difference to the behavior of the best-paid workers: their periods of convalescence grew 20 percent longer! For accidents that occurred *before* 15 July, these employees had been off work for an average of 4.3 weeks, but accidents that occurred *after* 15 July caused the same employees to stay home for an average of 5.2 weeks. Curiously, the average convalescence period for injured workers who were less well paid and thus unaffected by the rise in the upper limit stayed the same before and after 15 July. Nobody really believed that workplace accidents had suddenly become more serious for better-paid workers, and only for them, after 15 July 1980.[1]

Should we conclude that Kentucky employees at a certain pay grade are especially lacking in a sense of civic responsibility because of an individualism gone haywire that we would come across only in certain strata of American society? Certainly not. In France, the example of a change in the rules governing the parental education allowance tells us that French women, distinctly less well paid than the employees in Kentucky, who find themselves in comparable circumstances react in more or less the same way. The story, reduced to its essentials, is this: before 1994, the parental education allowance offered a monthly premium of around 3,000 francs ($600) to mothers with three children who agreed to leave the workforce. After 1994, this measure was extended to mothers with two children. The financial advantage of being in the workforce was therefore different for mothers with two children—and only for them— before and after 1994. It was found that the proportion of women in this group holding a job (their employment rate) went from 58.6 percent in March 1994 to 47.4 percent in March 1997, a fall of more than 11 percentage points in three years. The employment rate of mothers unaffected by the change made in 1994 *went up* by around three percentage points over the same period. So the drop in the employment rate of mothers with two children was considerable when contrasted with the prevailing pattern of workforce participation by women. Thomas Piketty, a researcher at the École des Hautes Études en Sciences Sociales, made a very detailed analysis of all the possible reasons for this fall in the employment rate of mothers with two children after 1994, and his unambiguous conclusion was that it was entirely due to the extension of the parental education allowance.[2]

These two examples simply instruct us that if being at work becomes less advantageous, fewer people *on average* will go to work. It is especially important to stress the words "on average" in the statement of this conclusion. These two stories do not say that *all* well-paid Kentucky employees who had a workplace accident after 15 July 1980 prolonged their convalescence, or that *all* French mothers with two children left the workforce after the extension of the parental education allowance; they tell us that there were *more* employees prolonging their convalescence rather than fewer, and that there were *more* mothers who gave up working after the extension of the parental education allowance rather than fewer. If Kentucky employees did not all react in the same way, that is because Kentucky employees are not all identical. If all French mothers with two children did not have the same reaction, that is because they are not all alike. Some earn high wages, and so the 3,000 franc premium was unlikely to interest them. But most earn modest wages; in March 1994 only 10 percent of the members of this category earned wages higher than 10,000 francs ($2,000) per month. Among these modestly paid mothers of families, some took the view that the social status conferred by holding a job was more important than the premium on offer, others took the view that to stop working (when their husbands were doing a good job as breadwinners) would give them a chance to try a different mode of family life, and so on.

While these two stories tell us that it is pointless to reason in terms of good or bad "citizenship" in the economic realm, they also instruct us that we must make a distinction between good and bad incentives. A good, or efficient, incentive leads to the goal sought; an inefficient one induces perverse effects that can sometimes run directly counter to the goal sought. The increase in the compensation payment for workplace accidents in the state of Kentucky was a bad incentive, since it aimed to maintain the purchasing power of the best-paid wage-earners, not to make their time off work last longer. On the other hand, the extension of the parental education allowance had the incentive effects desired, since its purpose was precisely to allow certain women to leave the workforce.[3]

We have just observed that certain persons have an incentive to work less, or even not at all, when working does not pay. In France, recipients of social support payments (for which we generally use the equivalent term "welfare" in this book) find themselves in this situation. They subsist on social transfers paid by the collectivity and can hope for no more than low wages if they do succeed in finding a job. For them, returning to work offers little or no financial advantage compared to what they receive on social assistance. The cost-benefit ratio is worsened by the expenses incurred in going to work (transportation, childcare, eventual tax on earned income, and so on). Such persons find themselves caught in an "inactivity trap."[4]

Does it pay to work in France?

In a study that appeared in 2002, two French scholars, Denis Anne and Yannick L'Horty, assessed in great detail the differences in the gain a person could derive from living solely on welfare, and the gain he could obtain if he found a job paid at minimum wage.[5] One of the original features of this study was that it took into account all the potential sources of support, national and local, for those with low incomes. There exist a host of local forms of assistance that, as their name indicates, are proper to each locality. The range of such assistance includes daycare centers; school meals; programs to cover the cost of transportation, of water, gas, and electricity bills, and of unpaid rent; vacation coupons; and vouchers for leisure activities. Since there are no statistics available for the whole range of such local assistance, Anne and L'Horty undertook their own survey in ten localities that reflected as closely as possible the geographic and economic diversity of France. They inventoried no less than 250 different forms of local social assistance. They then made calculations, for six different household configurations (single individual; one-parent family; childless couple; couple with one, two, or three children), of what each such household would be able to take in by combining, where that was possible, local assistance and aid from the national government. On average, the resources supplied by national aid amounted to €12,400 (about $14,000) per year. Local transfers added €3,400 (about $3,700) per year to that sum, or almost 21 percent of the total amount. For the couples with two or three children, such local assistance amounted to €4,400 (about $4,800) and €5,400 (about $6,000), respectively. Hence, a substantial quantity of social transfers is overlooked if local assistance is not taken into account.

Anne and L'Horty then attempted to answer the question, For each household configuration, how much time would it be necessary to work at the hourly minimum wage in order to take in *as much* as what combined local and national assistance could yield? Their results are summarized in figure 4.1.

We observe that it is couples with two children who have to work the longest if they hope to earn more than what social assistance can offer them. Starting from a baseline situation in which neither adult has any waged work, the total amount of time worked by the couple and paid at minimum wage would need to reach 44.5 hours per week for this couple to earn an income identical to what they could get from the combination of local and national assistance. In other words, a couple out of work with two children who succeeded in combining the local and national assistance to which they had a legitimate claim would lose money if one of them took a full-time job paid at minimum wage.[6] The

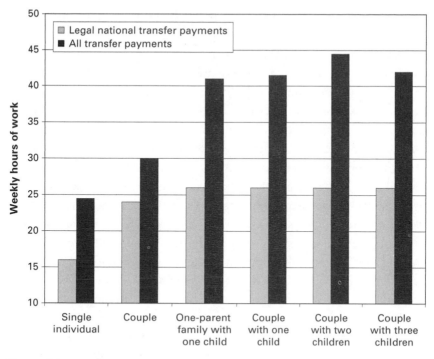

Figure 4.1
Weekly hours of work paid at minimum wage needed to earn an amount equal to local and national social assistance in France. Source: Denis Anne and Yannick L'Horty, "Transferts sociaux locaux et retour à l'emploi."

Interpretation: On average, a single individual can receive each week, without working, the equivalent of 16 hours at minimum wage if he or she is getting all the national assistance (or "transfer payments") to which he or she is legally entitled, and the equivalent of 24.5 hours paid at minimum wage if he or she is also getting local assistance.

same conclusion applies, in fact, to all households with at least one child. For all of them, a single full-time job at minimum wage leads to a loss of income. The childless couple barely escapes the same conclusion, since they would have to work for 30 hours (which is not far below the legal limit of full-time employment, 35 hours) in order not to suffer a loss of income. Only the single individual gets a significant financial advantage from taking a full-time job at minimum wage, because her income exceeds combined social assistance after 24 hours of work per week. On the other hand, neither the single individual nor any other household configuration gets any financial advantage by taking a half-time job paid at minimum wage.

The figures yielded by this study are difficult to ignore. Admittedly, it is rare for the same person to cumulate all the assistance to which he or she is entitled, but Anne and L'Horty point out that some unquantified forms of assistance, and certain loans available only to distinct socio-professional groups, have not been included, although they would have the effect of increasing the amount of assistance received. It is also the case that some of those whose main resource is welfare could neverthe-lesss obtain wages higher than the minimum wage. But these are mar-ginal cases: surveys carried out on recipients of the welfare program who do succeed in finding work indicate that, by a very large majority, their wages cluster around the monthly minimum wage for full-time jobs, and around half the monthly minimum wage for half-time jobs. Overall, the study gives a good idea of the lack of financial advantage, sometimes even the disadvantage, of holding a job paid at minimum wage for a great many recipients of welfare.

There is a policy, a simple one in principle, to reduce inactivity traps: the state can pay a wage supplement to all recipients of welfare if and only if they find a job. In other words, this policy aims to "make work pay." Such policies do not aim to solve the problem of unemployment or inactivity for *everyone* on welfare. The goal of policies that "make work pay" is twofold: on one hand, they try to influence the behavior of those who prefer idleness to work, and thus combat the inactivity trap; and on the other, they try to improve the situation of those who do find a job, and thus combat the poverty trap.

Policies to "make work pay" are not a miracle cure for all the ills of underemployment, for underemployment is sometimes the result of an insufficiency of job creation, as we pointed out in chapter 3. But if they are well thought out, such policies can be an efficient way of improving the outlook of substantial numbers of the unemployed and the inactive.

A Canadian experiment

In 1992 the provinces of New Brunswick and British Columbia decided to carry out a controlled experiment to discover whether offering a sub-stantial wage supplement to those who found a job would bring more people back to work. This experiment is of interest because it concerned only persons who were *already* hampered on the labor market: single-parent families who had been living for more than a year on basic welfare. From this population, a sample of 6,000 persons was drawn at random. The sample was highly representative: practically all those included were women, only one person out of nine had advanced beyond high school, almost 30 percent said they had physical or psychological problems, and virtually half had been clients of the welfare system for at least three years (much more than the minimum of 12 months necessary for inclusion in the experiment). This sample of 6,000 persons was again divided by a random draw into a test group and a control group of 3,000 persons each.

The experiment consisted of paying a premium, for a maximum of three years, to all members of the test group who found a job within the year following the starting date. This premium, paid monthly, was sizeable, for it practically *doubled* the pre-tax income of an employee making the minimum wage. There was one strict condition: the premium was offered only for full-time work (concretely, at least 30 hours per week), so as to privilege a complete exit from the welfare system. For this reason the experiment was called the Self-Sufficiency Project (SSP). In order to assess the effects of this measure to make work pay, members of the control group were observed in the normal condition of those looking for a job, meaning that no premium was paid to them if they did succeed in getting hired. Otherwise the 6,000 persons selected all had access to the same information from government employment agencies, whether they were in the test group or the control group.[7]

Figure 4.2 depicts the main findings of the SSP experiment. One month after it began, 9 percent of the members of both the test and control groups had a full-time job. One year on, 30 percent of the test group and 15 percent of the control group were working full-time. The difference of 15 percentage points between the two groups over a single year is a gauge of the impact of the premium, for it must be remembered that, according to the protocol of the SSP, the members of the test group receive a wage supplement only if they find a job *in less than a year.*

We note as well that the rate of employment of the test group holds at more or less the same level, in the region of 28 percent, starting from

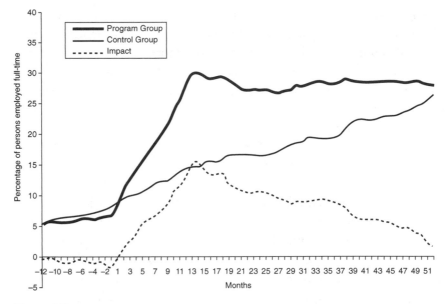

Figure 4.2
The results of the Self-Sufficiency Project. The boldface line indicates the percentage of persons in the test group holding a full-time job. The thin line indicates the percentage of persons in the control group holding a full-time job. Thirteen months after the start of the experiment, the percentage of persons in full-time employment was 30% in the test group and 15% in the control group. Source: Michalopoulos, ed., *Making Work Pay: Final Report on the Self-Sufficiency Project for Long Term Welfare Recipients.*

the fourteenth month, while the control group almost reaches this level at the end of the 54 months observed in the experiment. Hence, the test group "gains" around 40 months (more than three years) of employment compared to the control group, and so the premium did greatly accelerate the return to work. Given the difference of 15 points registered at the end of the first year, we can also deduce that a significant gap would have persisted between the two groups if the right to receive the premium had been extended to those who found a new job more than a year after the beginning of the experiment. It was also found that the wages received by the members of the control group and of the test group were the same at the end of the period observed in the experiment. The premium thus did not have the effect of lowering the remuneration offered to this category of persons.

Another result of the SSP experiment was to highlight the fundamental role of communication: all the participants received unambiguous messages from the organizers making it clear that the aim of the program was to favor their return to employment by "making work pay." Each member of the test group knew precisely what she would gain by finding a new job. This aspect of the Self-Sufficiency Project gave considerable impetus to its success.[8]

If we take into account the overall costs of the program (the wage supplements paid for three years to the members of the test group who found work, the administrative costs) and the overall gains (the difference between the sum of the wages received by the test group and that received by the control group, the savings realized by the welfare system), it is evident that the SSP experiment presented a positive balance for society. A study has even shown that the program was paying for itself through increased tax revenues.[9] The gains accruing to the collectivity are probably even greater than that, since various tests carried out on the children of the parents belonging to the test group have shown that their health and their cognitive abilities underwent some improvement over the whole course of the experiment. This point is worth underlining, for a full-time job automatically gives a single parent less time to take care of her children. But it would appear that having a job allows her to take better care of them.

It must be noted that this experiment did not offer the participants any particular help in the task of searching for a job. However, a parallel experiment, called SSP-Plus, was carried out on a sample of around 600 persons drawn at random; these were divided by a second random draw into a test group and a control group of 300 persons each. Both groups got the benefit of the same conditions offered to the test group in the general program; in other words, all 600 participants got a wage supplement if they found a full-time job, but the test group of 300 also received intensive job search assistance. Four years after the start of the experiment, the employment rate of the test group exceeded that of the control group by more than seven points. Job search assistance thus increases the effects of the financial incentive alone—a lesson worth remembering.

To sum up the key points, the SSP experiment instructs us that increasing the gap between the allowance a person will receive by staying unemployed and the income which he can expect to get by finding a job has a definite effect on his attitude. For one thing, this kind of policy shifts the threshold of "acceptability" of jobs. A job that would have been refused before because it was located too far away, or the wage was too low, or the hours were inconvenient, or for any other reason, now becomes acceptable. Another key finding is that, by increasing the gain from going to work, a policy of making work pay stimulates jobless persons to look harder for work. More of them begin doing so, and those who were already looking for work start to do so with greater zeal. Shifting the threshold of what is seen as an acceptable job and stimulating a more committed job search both lead to an accelerated rate of return to work, even, and perhaps especially, for persons who were having difficulty at the outset in getting hired.[10] One more thing is needed for this type of policy to succeed: it is not enough to make work pay; it has to be made to pay *a lot*. Behavior changes if the gains are substantial, not if they are marginal.

The Canadian experiment also reveals that we should not expect wondrous results from policies to make work pay. The acceleration of return to work was significant, but it was not observed in all, or even in the majority, of the participants in the experiment. Nevertheless, if such policies make it possible to increase the number of persons on welfare who do return to the labor market by 5 or 10 percentage points, then they have earned their place in the arsenal of policy options.

Negative income taxes

The Canadian experiment is not an isolated one. In order to combat the inactivity trap, many countries have put in place policies that increase the financial rewards flowing to low-wage employees. Such policies can take various forms. The most widespread one is the income tax credit, also called "negative income tax." In principle, it consists of granting reductions in tax to those who accept poorly paid work. The reduction can be calibrated in such a way that it exceeds the amount of tax that would have been owed, and the tax authorities pay the difference directly to the person concerned, whence the expression "*negative* income tax." The United States has had a tax of this type in place since 1975, called the "earned income tax credit" (EITC). It is targeted at households with few means in which at least one person is working, and especially households with one or more children. The EITC grants very substantial income supplements for certain categories of household: it can increase the income of households with at least two children, where just one adult is working full-time at minimum wage, by around 40 percent. When both adults in a household with at least two children are working full-time at minimum wage, the EITC remains significant, for it still yields the equivalent of one-tenth of the total household income. The amount of the EITC falls to zero for households with at least two children when both parents are working full-time at the median wage. And the tax credit falls off sharply for childless households, whatever their resources. At the end of the 1990s, around one household in five was benefiting from the EITC, which represents 20,000,000 households.[11]

The United Kingdom has also experimented with the negative income tax since the end of the 1970s. In its latest guise, introduced in 1999, it goes by the name "working families tax credit" (WFTC). This is an income tax credit applied to households with children, the youngest of whom is under 19 years of age, and in which at least one person works. Since income tax is deducted at source in the United Kingdom, this credit has the advantage of being shown directly on the pay slip, in the form of either a wage supplement or a lower tax rate. The requirements for eligibility and the modes of calculating the amounts paid are highly complex, but the tax credit proves to be very important for the most disadvantaged households. It can markedly exceed the direct wage: a household in which one adult works 16 hours per week at the hourly rate of £3.60 takes in a gross weekly wage income of £57.60, while the credit is much more than that at £92. In this case, the assistance given represents 160 percent of gross income! So the WFTC is more generous than the EITC, but it is also more narrowly targeted, since only one household in twenty benefits from it.[12]

The negative income tax, like all measures to make work pay, aims to attract onto the labor market persons who, without this measure, would see little or no financial advantage in holding a job. But it runs the risk of producing effects that run counter to this goal. For married couples, the negative income tax, by augmenting their joint income, might give one of them an incentive to cut back on her hours of work, or even give up her job (to take care of the children, for example), which would evidently be paradoxical. But assessments carried out in the United States and the United Kingdom show that this risk is not a real threat, even if the EITC and the WFTC do in fact have a tendency to slightly diminish the average amount of time worked by persons holding a job. Thus, according to a report of the Institute for Fiscal Studies, London, the WFTC increased employment among single parents by around 3.6 percentage points, while for couples with children it had no significant effect on mothers' employment. In total, the employment gains are estimated at between 25,000 and 59,000 extra jobs.[13] In the United States, the employment rate of single women with one or more children in their care increased in the course of the 1990s. But it is the employment rate of the poorest 25 percent of them—precisely those who benefited the most from the income supplements paid by the EITC—that rose the most, going from 30 percent at the start of the decade to 50 percent at its close. According to the estimates of David Ellwood of Harvard University, we may attribute one-third of this rise (seven percentage points all the same) to measures that aim to make work pay. The other two-thirds flow from the improvement of the economic situation overall and from other reforms to the fiscal and welfare systems.[14] Hence the negative income tax played an important part in the increase in employment among the most disadvantaged single women. Various evaluations also indicate that if the income tax credit introduced is not sufficiently generous, it will not make a strong impact on the labor market participation of poorly educated persons.

Since 30 May 2001, France too has had a negative income tax, which bears the evocative name "premium for employment" (*prime pour l'emploi*, or PPE). This is a tax credit flowing to persons whose income from wages—meaning they have to have worked to benefit from it—lies in the range from 0.3 to 1.4 times the minimum wage. Thus it affects about one household in four. The PPE was introduced for laudable reasons, yet it has been set up in a disappointing way that appears to negate its core impact on employment.[15] For one thing, both the law and the relevant schedule of calculations are frightfully complex. For another, the maximum amounts of the premium are very modest, and in any case markedly smaller than those of the EITC and the WFTC. They come to less than 5 percent of declared income, a figure that contrasts strongly with those of the EITC and the WFTC, for which the maximum amounts of assistance represent respectively almost 40 percent and 160 percent of declared income.[16]

In contrast to its American and British counterparts, the negative income tax *à la française* is not particularly targeted at households with one or more children. For these households it does stipulate some supplemental payments, but relatively small ones. Thus the "target" is a wide swath of the population: practically one household out of four can benefit. In its present form, the PPE distributes small amounts of money to a great many people, which means that in the end its costs are very high. France has not yet grasped that the main lesson of the experience of other countries is that it is necessary to make work pay—and pay well—if financial incentives are to have any significant impact on labor market participation and returns to employment. As a result, all such policies are costly, and the manner in which they are financed demands closer scrutiny.

Tax the "rich"?

When we confront the problem of financing public expenditure, there is always someone ready to propose the miracle solution: make the "rich" pay! This approach is generally rejected with the argument that it would cause the most effective persons to move abroad, leading in the end to a reduction in the national wealth. In France, the example of the best soccer players fleeing to countries that have lower tax rates is frequently adduced to illustrate the perverse effects of increased fiscal pressure on high incomes. Arthur Laffer, one of President Reagan's economic advisers, even asserted that increases in taxes beyond a certain limit end by *reducing* economic activity and *diminishing* the tax take.

Many studies carried out in the last decade have considerably advanced our understanding of the relevance of the famous "Laffer effect."[17] Jon Gruber and Emmanuel Saez have analyzed the consequences of the tax reductions introduced by the Reagan administration in the United States in the 1980s.[18] Since these reductions did not affect all income brackets in the same manner, it is possible to pinpoint their impact by comparing changing patterns in the income of persons whose tax rate went down only slightly with corresponding patterns in the case of those who got larger tax reductions. Gruber and Saez show that a rise in the rates of tax on the highest incomes alters the behavior of those earning these incomes. They find that persons making more than $100,000 per year pay *less* tax when their tax rate rises, which means either that they have cut back on their activity, or that they have shifted part of it offshore.[19] This result is not surprising. Persons with high incomes are generally highly qualified and have substantial savings. Thus they can work less, or do as the soccer players do and expatriate, taking their savings with them. Thomas Piketty undertook a similar exercise for high-income earners in France over the period 1970–1996, focusing on the 1 percent of households that have the highest incomes.[20] He finds that, in this population, the tax take has little sensitivity to changes in the rates. The tax take would only begin to fall off if the tax rate were to rise above 80 percent, which far exceeds the highest rate of income tax (which is around 50 percent).[21]

We can draw two important conclusions from this research:

1. The Laffer effect does indeed exist, but for very high tax rates. Thus it is inefficient to impose excessively high tax rates that reduce the tax take. However, any reduction in taxes that leads to a reduction in the tax take limits the possibilities of redistributing income and combating inequality.

2. Increases in income tax only yield substantial resources if they affect a sufficiently large population. For instance, in France today only 1 percent of households have an income greater than €8,000 (around $6,700) per month, and these households aggregate around 8 percent of the overall income of the French economy.[22] To take 10 percent more tax on income brackets greater than €8,000 per month (which is a lot) would produce an increase in the tax take on the order of 0.02 percent of GDP (which is not a lot). Making the rich pay yields little. Moreover, Thomas Piketty points out that a Laffer effect might well materialize if the rate rise were pushed even higher than this extra 10 percent. In that case, the tax increase would be highly counterproductive, since it would lead to a diminution of the tax take. The margin of maneuver when it

comes to increasing fiscal resources by taking more from very rich households exclusively is therefore very restricted. The moral of this line of reasoning is that the very rich are not rich enough; or that there are not enough very rich persons for an increase in the tax on their income to really improve the state of public finances.

We have emphasized repeatedly that the mobility of high incomes constitutes an important boundary to the possibilities of redistribution. Now, in most industrialized countries we have been witnessing for almost a decade a trend to lower the tax rates on the highest incomes. This in turn is part of a larger trend toward "fiscal competition," in which each country tries to attract individuals with the highest incomes by offering an attractive fiscal climate. A vicious circle thus comes into being, in which everyone is obliged to lower their taxes because the others are doing so. Finding the budgetary resources that ambitious redistributive policies require would necessitate an escape from this vicious circle through international coordination of fiscal policies, in particular within the European Union. That is not the direction in which things are moving at present.

Making work pay is a necessary condition for the creation and survival of jobs. It is a condition just as necessary as holding down the cost of labor, which we looked at in the preceding chapter. We have seen that it is possible to make work pay through fiscal systems inspired by the negative income tax, while also keeping the cost of low-skilled labor under control thanks to payroll tax relief. These policies should be pursued, and directed more accurately at those who need them most.[23] But such policies do not, in themselves, guarantee the smooth functioning of a labor market in constant mutation. Managing these mutations is a task that cannot be accomplished solely by keeping the cost of manpower under control plus incentives to participate in the labor market. So we have to ensure that movements in employment are efficient, and manage uncertainty. This is the purpose of unemployment insurance, job protection legislation, and policies to promote training—the topics we will treat in the following chapters.

5

The Utility of Unemployment

The enormous dimensions of the movements of manpower in most of the industrialized countries cause one of the most familiar job descriptions in our societies to be that of "job-seeker." The job of looking for work is one of the most profitable for society as a whole. It ensures the reallocation of the labor force toward the most efficient jobs, and thus constitutes an essential source of growth.[1] The search for a job is thus an economically useful activity; it should be remunerated as such.

This is not the common view. Unemployment is most often seen as one of the worst of the evils of which our societies cannot rid themselves. Such a conception colors some systems of insurance against the effects of unemployment profoundly, that of France in particular. It orients them toward a logic of assistance, in which the unemployed person is regarded primarily as a victim who must, above all, be supplied with a decent income. This objective should not be abandoned, but in isolation it has perverse effects. The second objective of unemployment insurance should be to supply the recipient with help and incentives in finding a new job. If no attempt is made to meet this goal, the social utility of movements of manpower is undercut, and the result is to perpetuate an excessively high level of unemployment—a source of exclusion and inequality.

The job of being unemployed

At every moment there are simultaneously very large numbers of unemployed persons looking for work, and employers with positions vacant who are looking for personnel to fill them. For instance, in January 2005, there were about 3.5 million job openings in the United States and 7.7

million unemployed workers.[2] The simultaneous presence of immense numbers of vacant jobs and job-seekers in most trades signifies that a "match" (meaning an encounter between an employer and a job seeker that ends with a hire) is not as easy to bring about as one might think. The reason is that, today even more than in the past, a match remains very specific. A maintenance worker does not accept just any job offer falling within his area of competence; many factors guide his choice. The location of the job is obviously one, but there is also the wage offered, the working conditions, the work schedule, the general reputation of the company, the career outlook, and so on. Reciprocally, an employer looking for a maintenance worker does not necessarily hire the first person who comes along. She may take into account the candidate's professional experience, the fit between the tasks she wants to see accomplished and what she thinks the candidate can do, the candidate's adaptability to unanticipated operations and ability to mesh with the routines and rules proper to the firm, even the sympathy or antipathy she may feel at first contact.

Naturally all this information is not known at the moment when the job seeker and the employer launch their respective searches. The aim of these searches is precisely to bring to light such information, which is unknown at the outset or known to only one of the protagonists. The principal activity of a job seeker is a quest for information, and that quest takes time, sometimes even quite a lot of time. At the end of 2005, the average duration of unemployment was around 18 weeks in the United States and around 15 months in France!

These lengthy spells testify to the many obstacles a job-seeker encounters in looking for work. One is struck to find that many employers also declare that they run into difficulty in recruiting the personnel they need. For example, in France a survey of 12,000 firms in 2000 indicates that 36 percent of companies *who wanted to hire* gave up on the effort to do so (at least temporarily).[3] It also shows that these difficulties affect business sectors with different degrees of intensity. The construction sector has the hardest time, with 59 percent of companies having given up trying to hire at times when they wished to do so. The lowest figure is 26 percent, in the finance and real estate sector and in that of services to business. Thus, there are not, in general, "job shortages," but there are always obstacles to matching—which is not the same thing.

The obstacles to matching are summed up by the ratio between the number of job-seekers and the number of jobs vacant. For example, if there are 14 job offers for butchers for every 10 requests, and 7 job offers for maintenance workers for every 10 requests, unemployed butchers ought to have less difficulty in finding a job than maintenance workers who are also looking. On average, a butcher stays unemployed for less time than a maintenance worker. But neither one can avoid making an energetic search effort. Many studies have focused on the conditions for making this search as efficient as possible for the job-seeker and society as a whole. A very short search is not necessarily a sign of greater efficiency, for the quality of the resulting matches may be rather low, which does nothing to raise the quantity and quality of the overall production of goods and services, and thus the "well-being" of the average citizen. Such poor matches can happen when unemployment insurance pays too little. When that is the case, job-seekers are prepared to accept jobs that do not suit them: they have no other choice if they are to meet their most elementary needs. Daron Acemoglu of the Massachusetts Institute of Technology and Robert Shimer of Princeton University believe that the U.S. economy suffered from this failing in the 1990s.[4] During that decade, the unemployment rate and the average spell of looking for work were particularly low and short. According to their simulations, a (small) increase in the spell of unemployment would have been beneficial for the average consumer. It would certainly have increased the number of job-seekers, but the improvement in the quality of the matches would have compensated for this negative effect. The result would have been a palpable increase in the productivity of work, and that in turn would have allowed the overall production of goods and services to increase in the long run.

We should not conclude on the basis of this simulation that very long spells of unemployment are a sign that things are in good shape. No study backs up that idea. Countries where the duration of unemployment is very long do not have productivity superior to that of others. Quite the contrary: a prolonged duration of unemployment reveals the fundamental ineffectiveness of the institutions guiding the job search. The experience of many countries tells us that it is perfectly possible to make job searches more effective. They also show us how to go about it.

Compensation for unemployment and the duration of unemployment

Unemployment insurance is often criticized from opposing points of view. On the one hand, there are many who maintain that the benefits are too small and the benefit period too brief. On the other, there are those who claim to know job-seekers who do not really hunt for work as long as they are getting their benefits, and they conclude that the system is too generous. The relevant research shows that these positions are not as contradictory as they might appear at first.

One way to find out if unemployed persons are taking selfish advantage of unemployment insurance is to observe their behavior at the moment when their benefits run out.[5] If all of them immediately find jobs when the payments stop, we may suspect that they could have exited from unemployment sooner. Many studies have illustrated the impact of reduced income on returns to work. Their strategy is to utilize surveys from which it is possible to calculate the proportion of unemployed persons who find new jobs as a function of how long they have been unemployed. A study of the French labor market at the end of the 1980s and in the 1990s by Brigitte Dormont, Denis Fougère, and Ana Prieto gives a good picture of the results obtained in this domain.[6] They are shown in figure 5.1, which indicates the proportion of unemployed persons who find jobs every day as a function of how long they have been unemployed. The vertical bar at fourteen months corresponds to the moment at which unemployed persons come to the end of their period of insurance and so must face a drop in income. The graph on the top relates to persons receiving the lowest wages (situated in the first quartile of the distribution), and the one on the bottom relates to those with the highest wages (situated in the last quartile of the distribution). Both show clearly that returns to work accelerate as the termination of entitlement to unemployment insurance approaches.

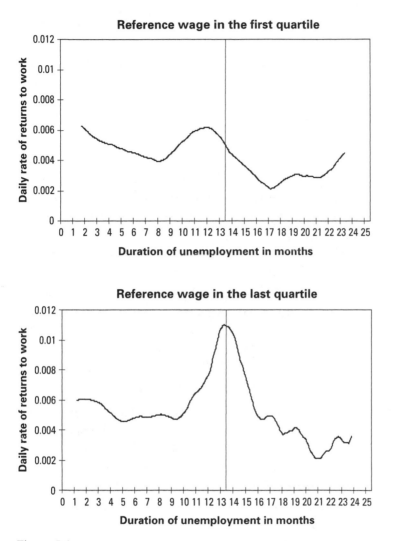

Figure 5.1
Rate of return to work in France between 1986 and 1992 for individuals over 25 years old. Source: Dormont, Fougère, and Prieto, "The Effect of the Time Profile of Unemployment Insurance Benefits on Exit from Unemployment."

More generally, studies on the effects of benefits paid to the unemployed highlight three main points.

1. A drastic reduction in the amount of unemployment insurance does drive some workers to find a new job quickly. Thus, there are some unemployed persons who do not really look for work or accept job offers until the end of their period of entitlement to these payments.[7]

2. The positive impact of the termination of entitlement on the return to work is most prominent for the most skilled individuals, who receive the largest insurance payments. We see that their rate of exit from unemployment doubles as the termination of their entitlement approaches (the bottom graph), whereas that of persons who earn the lowest remuneration increases only by half (the top graph). Highly skilled persons enjoy a wider margin of maneuver, which lets them take maximum advantage of the income from unemployment insurance.

3. Some of the unemployed do not find jobs after the fourteenth month, when unemployment insurance falls off steeply. Past this stage, the rate of return to employment is lower than the one that prevails before the termination of entitlement. So there exists a significant proportion of unemployed persons who have little chance of finding work, independent of the amount of unemployment insurance they receive.

What these results tell us above all is that the population of the unemployed is very heterogeneous. There are doubtless some who take advantage of the system, and others who follow the rules. Those who do not actively look for employment do so to the detriment of the others. If they exited sooner from unemployment, it would be possible to compensate the most indigent persons better for the same overall cost. Rather than "starving" all the unemployed, we must try to work out a just and effective system, remunerating and guiding the search for a job. In this regard, a look at the historical experience of trade unions at the end of the nineteenth century has something to teach us.

A mutual commitment

The existence of trade unions (*syndicats professionels*) was recognized in France by a law passed on 21 March 1884. Article 6 of this law stated that they "can freely create and administer offices supplying information about offers of, and requests for, work." The role of the placement agency thus comes immediately to the fore. Note that there was no question of co-management by employers and employees: the placement function was managed and financed by the trade unions alone; the employers did not take part. The richest trade unions had permanent delegates at the end of the nineteenth century, charged with the task of coordinating offers of work and requests for it, but these cases were unusual. Gradually, the services of assembling information and assisting placement were taken over by institutions called *bourses de travail* (labor exchanges), which served all the trade unions within the same geographic area. The *bourse de travail* for Paris started up in 1887.

The example of the powerful printing trade federation (*Fédération du livre*) illustrates well how this role of placement agency was conceived. The basic principle was simple: support was paid to unemployed members only after a rigorous check had been made on their efforts to find a job. At the end of the nineteenth century, this support mainly took the form of travel money, called a *viaticum*, which enabled workers without employment to visit a locality long enough to call on the local printshops and, if they did not succeed in getting hired there, to move on to a neighboring locality. The right to receive the *viaticum* was subject to drastic conditions. In particular, one had to have paid one's dues to the *Fédération du livre* regularly; and a worker who quit his job voluntarily received nothing for the first two months (an eternity at that period) after quitting. The amount of the *viaticum* depended on the distance the member had to travel, and was paid by the day.

The *Fédération du livre* employed specialized personnel called secretaries whose task was to check on the efforts made by these unemployed "travelers." Article 30 of the Federation's regulations spells out the content of these checks:

A standard form, containing the names of all the printshops in the city, will be given to the traveler by the secretary. This form, signed by the foreman of each shop, must be returned to the secretary to prove that the member did visit all the printshops in the locality. After this form has been handed over [to the member], a departure visa will be stamped in his official record book. Traveling members must not have any dealings with workplaces before they have reported to the person in charge of the *viaticum* or a member of the bureau of the section, on penalty of losing their *viaticum*.[8]

As we see, the job search efforts of the unemployed man were rigorously checked. The secretary of the union supplied him with a list of all the employers in the locality that he was to visit. He could not start looking without informing the secretary first. If he didn't succeed in getting hired in that locality, he received a new *viaticum* for travel to another locality only after he furnished proof that he did indeed visit all the printshops in the city in question. The possibility of losing the *viaticum* is made explicit.

The *viaticum* must be distinguished from compensation for unemployment properly speaking. The latter was paid to a worker who was without work or sick, but who wanted to find another job without moving somewhere else. Thus it could not be combined with the *viaticum*. The conditions for getting this compensation were just as punctilious. In order to be entitled, one had to be a member with no dues in arrears for at least a year. The duration of eligibility for the payments was a function of the number of years of uninterrupted membership in the union. For a member without a job to have the right to receive this compensation, the *involuntary* character of his job loss had to be established by a written declaration from the owner of the establishment where he had been working; and this declaration had to be certified by one or more members of the union working in the same establishment. Moreover, article 43 of the statutes of the Federation specify that "unemployed persons, except for members who are ill, must . . . accept any position indicated to them. . . . Any unemployed person refusing to report to the position indicated to him, or who, through negligence, abandons or loses this position, will be deprived of his right to compensation for fifteen days following the job offer. Unemployed members are required to sign in [at the union offices] . . . every day."[9]

In other words, the whole process of searching for a job was entirely overseen by the union, leaving the unemployed member very little personal initiative. It is counterintuitive that a system placing so many restrictions on its own members could have been conceived and managed by a workers' union. Such complete supervision of the unemployed made it possible, by excluding any unauthorized steps on their part, to maintain and even increase the level of wages in the printing trades. Apart from that motive, the thing to remember from this historical example is that compensation was only paid within the framework of a mutual commitment. The placement agency (the union, in the case at hand) supplied the unemployed person with real help, and he for his part was obliged to carry out the job search required of him. The union assisted the job-seeker by indicating potential employers to him, and the job-seeker was then obliged to go for an interview within a limited timeframe or suffer a penalty.

The most effective systems of unemployment insurance in the modern world follow this principle of mutual commitment. A look at what two small European countries, Switzerland and the Netherlands, have achieved in this area will allow us to spell out how this contractual principle is actually applied. We will see that, in essence, a *credible* system of checking on the job search activity of an unemployed person is necessary. But this condition is by no means sufficient. If the public employment services do not fulfill their part of the bargain, which consists of furnishing real help to job-seekers, and content themselves with simply checking on them, then the system loses all effectiveness.

Switzerland: The importance of credibility

In Switzerland, as elsewhere, payment of the compensation provided for by the unemployment insurance system is subject to conditions of eligibility. Concretely, one must have paid in contributions for at least six months out of the two years preceding the date on which one is registered as unemployed. But this condition is waived for those who have just graduated from the school system or come out of prison, and for men and women who have been looking after their offspring. Compared to those of the other OECD countries, the payments are relatively generous, in the range of 70 to 80 percent of the last wage earned. One may receive them for two years. After that, the unemployed person is taken under the wing of the welfare system, which is also relatively generous; for example, an unmarried person without resources loses no more than 25 percent of her benefit by moving from the insurance system to the welfare system.

Throughout the period of unemployment, the payment of the benefit is subject to precise conditions. Every month, the unemployed person is required to supply details of "suitable" jobs for which she has applied. The notion of a suitable job is based on several criteria, such as being not more than two hours distant from the person's home and offering a wage equal to at least two-thirds of the last wage she received. Potential jobs can be found by the unemployed person herself or proposed to her by the public employment service. The latter also sets the minimum number of monthly applications which the job-seeker must make.

The job search activity of the unemployed person is monitored by the same member of the staff of the public employment service. The unemployed person must meet this staff member at least once a month for an assessment of her activity and the drafting of a plan of future action. In addition, she must agree to enter any training program to which she may be assigned.

If the job-seeker fails to meet any or all of these obligations, she receives a notification requiring her to justify this failure within a short time (around two weeks). This notification also sets out the penalty she will incur if the reasons supplied are not judged to be valid. The penalty consists of a suspension of the benefit payment for a period that varies according to the reason for it. If the job-seeker has not respected the minimum number of applications required, the suspension may last from one to 15 days. But it can rise to 30 days if she does not show up at the monthly meeting, and even 60 days if she has turned down a "suitable" job.

Let us review the essential features of the Swiss system of unemployment insurance: high payments (both from the insurance system proper and from the welfare system); a precise definition of what constitutes a "suitable" job; the obligation to apply for such jobs; intensive personalized assistance (at least one meeting per month) in order to assess the effort made already and plan steps for the future; and finally, an explicit statement of the penalties that will apply in case commitments are not met. Faced with all these stringencies, one may wonder whether they are really necessary. The answer is that they are.

The efficiency of this system, which unites intensive personalized help with credible sanctions, has been demonstrated by research which exploits the fact that the unemployment insurance system is decentralized, with the effective management being carried out at the local agencies. The result is a certain variation in the application of penalties; this arises from the fact that each canton interprets federal law differently, and has its own administrative procedures and "culture." For example, in December 1998 in Switzerland as a whole, 19 unemployed persons out of every thousand were penalized. But some cantons inflicted no penalties, while one canton penalized 91 job-seekers out of every thousand. Using very detailed files describing the outcomes of all those who became unemployed between September 1997 and March 1998, and were followed until May 1999, a team of researchers from the universities of Zurich and Tilburg took advantage of these variations in local management to evaluate the effects of the different facets of the Swiss unemployment insurance system.[10] Utilizing the variable frequency of notifications and of penalties actually imposed, and taking into account the individual histories of the unemployed persons, they were able to construct an indicator of the *credibility* of the penalty system proper to each agency. If he has not met his obligations, a job-seeker registered with an agency where the indicator is high has a better chance of being penalized than he would if he were registered with an agency where the indicator is low.

The results of this study are unambiguous: the higher the degree of credibility attached to the penalties, the higher the rate of exits from unemployment. That means that a job-seeker registered with an agency where the credibility indicator of the penalties is high spends less time unemployed on average than one supervised by an agency with a weak indicator. Note that this conclusion concerns *all* the unemployed, not just the ones who were actually penalized. The credibility of the penalties has a positive effect on all the actors. It influences the behavior of the job-seekers, but also that of the staff of the employment service, whose responsibility toward their clients becomes greater and who are therefore more motivated. The efficiency of the whole process of the job search is improved.

The possibility of actually being penalized makes the whole system credible. There is an illuminating analogy with the behavior of motorists. Setting a speed limit, when everyone knows that it will seldom if ever be enforced robs it of all credibility. The system remains ineffective: no one respects the speed limit, and the number of deaths on the road climbs. If, however, the chance of being caught for speeding is high *and* if the fines for doing so are applied, most drivers will adapt their behavior in consequence. There will be fewer deaths on the road . . . and fewer drivers will be fined.

The effect of credibility in the system of checking is confirmed by other studies. In the United Kingdom, researchers tested the impact of a supplementary interview, compulsory on pain of penalty, between a job-seeker and the staffer in charge of her file, within the framework of the Restart program set up at the end of the 1980s. They carried out a controlled experiment by comparing the behavior of job-seekers who were summoned to this supplementary interview (the test group) and others who were not (the control group). It was found that the rate of exit from unemployment rose strongly in the test group *after* its members received the letter informing them of the obligation to turn up at this extra interview, and explaining the entire structure of assistance, checking, and penalties they would undergo in the program, but *before* the first interview had even taken place.[11] An American study carried out on the basis of files on exits from unemployment in the state of Kentucky between October 1994 and June 1996 comes to the same conclusion: the rate of exit from unemployment rises significantly in the interval of time between receipt of a letter summoning job-seekers to an interview and the date of the interview if it is compulsory and attended by penalties.[12]

The Netherlands: On the ineffectiveness of penalties on their own

In the Netherlands, to benefit from the unemployment insurance regime, one must have worked at least 26 weeks out of the 39 preceding the date on which one registers as unemployed. Those who are not eligible for this status receive 70 percent of minimum wage for six months, and an unemployed person who has exhausted his insurance entitlement is taken in hand by a welfare system and given an allowance that varies with the income of the household. For job-seekers who do qualify for unemployment insurance, the payout amounts to 70 percent of the last wage earned, and the period of time over which it is paid depends on the amount of time the job-seeker previously worked. Roughly speaking, each 10-year period of work entitles one to a single year of unemployment insurance. When entitlement ends, the unemployed person can still receive 70 percent of minimum wage for two years (if he was under 57.5 years old the day he became unemployed).

As in Switzerland, the search for a job takes place under precisely codified conditions. An unemployed person must actively look for work, and must accept any *suitable* job offer. She is also obliged to take part in any training programs that the public employment service orders her to attend. She must submit a *weekly* report stating the search efforts she has made (emailed reports are accepted). Every month she has an interview with the staff member in charge of her file. On that occasion, the staffer checks that all obligations have been met. If they have not, a reduction in the insurance payment may be imposed (this is not automatic), lowering the payment on average by 10 percent for two months. But, on a case by case basis, the penalties can be greater than that.

The first contact with the employment service takes place three days after the first insurance installment (very soon, therefore). This is an interview around 45 minutes long, in which the person's CV is reviewed, along with letters expressing interest in particular jobs, the different ways in which a job might be found, and so on. It concludes with a plan of action which the job-seeker must follow until the next meeting. The frequency of these interviews with an employment service staff member is monthly at a minimum. Each interview lasts about 20 minutes, during which actions taken are assessed and a plan for the coming month formulated. This process does not go on longer, in principle, than six months.

During the first interview the job-seekers are classified—"profiled," in the jargon of the employment service—into one of four categories. The classification criteria are in part objective (age, experience, education), and in part subjective: general self-presentation, ability to speak good Dutch, putative readiness to carry out a job search, etc. Type I comprises those who ought not to have particular problems finding a new job. Into types II and III fall those who lack the necessary qualifications, and who should be steered into suitable training programs. Finally, those persons most remote from the prospect of employment and who require particular help are classified as type IV. Note that 60 percent of unemployed persons fall into type I.

A study carried out on the basis of data from the Netherlands suggests that the combination of personalized assistance and credible sanctions notably improves the employment prospects of type II and III persons.[13] An experiment performed in a local employment agency made the picture sharper. It aimed to evaluate the effectiveness of the checking done on the search activity of the type I unemployed. First a test group and a control group were drawn. The normal regime described above was applied to the test group, whereas for the control group, contact with the employment service took place *only* by mail. Thus, the control group automatically got less help and was checked on less thoroughly than the test group, since the obligation to meet periodically with employment service staff was dropped. No significant difference in the frequency of exits from unemployment was observed between the two groups, thus casting doubt on the usefulness of help and checking, or at least of a portion of these activities. Still, inquiries among members of the test group revealed that the amount of help and supportive attention given to job-seekers was very low anyway in the agency where the experiment was carried out. Essentially, the staff did no more than verify the obligations of the persons in their charge.[14] In other words, very little help was given to unemployed persons in this agency, and the experiment showed ultimately that, in such conditions, the intensity of the checking had practically no influence on the behavior of job-seekers. The conclusion to be drawn is that a system of checking and penalties *without* significant supportive help for the unemployed can lose all effectiveness.

The United States has carried out numerous experiments of this kind since the start of the 1980s. Their conclusions are essentially in agreement with the ones we have just highlighted. For example, the Nevada Claimant Placement Program, which was tried in 1977–1978 in Nevada, supplied members of the test group with more frequent personalized assistance delivered by permanent staff, who also made stricter checks on job search activity. The result observed was that the average duration of unemployment was shorter by more than three weeks in the test group (an appreciable gain for the United States, where the average duration of a job hunt has fluctuated over time between three and five months). The experiment was repeated ten years later under the name Nevada Claimant Employment Program with similar conditions. The average duration of unemployment in the test group was still lower than that of the control group, but this time only by a little less than two weeks. As a general rule, all the experiments carried out in the United States during the 1980s indicate that checking on the job-seekers' effort combined with help in the job search results in a lowering of the duration of unemployment with no significant effect on hiring wages, which would seem to indicate that there was no degradation in the quality of the matches: job-seekers reduced their search time without taking worse jobs.[15]

In some western European countries, the trade unions that represent workers are most reluctant to accept the idea of integrating (other than in theory) the principle of mutual commitment into the system of unemployment insurance. Probably this is because in such countries an unemployed person is thought of as being more like someone afflicted with a serious illness than a person who is still a participant in economic life. If the unemployed person is thought of purely as a sufferer, then society owes her its help, in the hope that she will get better soon. Nothing more. This is not the right way to think of the unemployed person. Periods of unemployment are part of the normal course of events in economic life. By making possible better matches between job-seekers and firms, they are of benefit to the collectivity. Every period of unemployment ought to be viewed as a period of *workforce participation* of a particular kind— the search for the best match possible—which should profit the individual concerned, but from which the collectivity as a whole likewise benefits. The work of looking for employment is *socially* useful, and it is normal (and profitable) that the job-seeker's material needs should be taken care of by the collectivity. Thus, there are good reasons for him to be remunerated properly. But it is also normal (and profitable) for the collectivity to attempt to make this job search activity as efficient as possible. That requires binding mutual commitments on the part of the public or private agencies and their unemployed clients.

The reduction of the risks of working life in an environment characterized by high uncertainty must be grounded in a generous unemployment insurance program that puts into practice the principle of mutual commitment. Still, real security in working life cannot be attained except by giving coherent support not just to the effort to find employment, but also to decisions about the creation and destruction of jobs. As we shall see in the next chapter, job protection legislation is necessary, but it must be carefully codified.

6

Protecting Employment

In November 2005, the Weyerhaeuser Company's pulp and paper plant in Plymouth, North Carolina, announced plans to stop manufacturing the cardboard used to make boxes, and to lay off about 200 employees in January 2006. The layoffs will reduce the workforce at the plant to 750, down from 1,300 three years earlier. Officials from Washington and from surrounding counties promised to make vigorous efforts to put the unemployed workers in touch with companies looking to hire, but it didn't occur to anyone to haul Weyerhaeuser before the courts. Elsewhere, though, laying off workers is not so straightforward.

In July 1999 one of the companies in the Michelin group laid off 451 persons at its Wolber plant in the French city of Soissons. Two months later, the management announced a rise of 20 percent in half-yearly profits. The workers took the matter to an industrial tribunal, and in February 2002 the Michelin group was ordered to pay damages and interest amounting to €10 million, on the grounds that what Europeans call "economic layoffs"[1] are justified in order to *preserve* the competitiveness of a firm or of the group to which it belongs, but not in order to *improve* it.

The cases of the Weyerhaeuser Company or the Michelin group are not exceptional. Around 30,000 wage-earners lose or leave their jobs every working day in France, and the number in the United States is 250,000. These examples illustrate two diametrically opposed types of employment protection legislation. In the United States, the law leaves the employer a relatively free hand, but in certain countries of western Europe, especially France, employers are subject to strict controls, based on review by a judge and, where appropriate, countermeasures in the form of damages, interest, and penal sanction. In this chapter we maintain that such an approach is both inequitable and inefficient: inequitable because it protects certain wage-earners, who are far from being the most disadvantaged ones on average, while heightening the insecurity of other, less favored, workers; and inefficient because it does nothing to shore up the overall volume of employment. On the contrary, all the empirical information at our disposal indicates that legislation of this kind may temporarily avoid certain job destructions, but does so at an exorbitant cost that degrades the financial health of firms and reduces total employment. This does not mean that it is pointless to try to protect employment. On the contrary, it is indispensable to do so; but it is a task that must be addressed on meaningful economic foundations.

The goals of employment protection

In the United States, the Equal Employment Opportunity (EEO) laws serve primarily to protect wage-earners against violations of their work contract that do not respect the fundamental rights of the person. These laws prohibit discrimination in most workplaces on the basis of age, sex, ethnic or national origin, disability, and veteran status. In France, likewise, the preamble to the Constitution of 1946 ordains that "no one may suffer injury, in his work or employment, by reason of his origins, his opinions, or his beliefs." The labor code inspired by this preamble stipulates that any job loss must be motivated by "a real and serious cause." It must, in particular, have nothing to do with place of origin, sex, morality, family situation, nationality, ethnicity, race, religion, state of health, handicap (except where duly certified by an occupational health physician), pregnancy, participation in a legal strike, opinions uttered within the bounds protected by employees' right of free expression, political choice, membership in a union, and so on. To fire someone in disregard of these stipulations is to commit an offense, and may give rise to penal sanctions and the payment of damages and interest.

Such protection of fundamental rights is not seriously opposed by anyone, and forms an integral part of the legislation of all the industrialized countries. But very often, measures to protect employment go much farther, to the extent of regulating all the procedures by which a worker joins and leaves a firm. They provide for an official review of the "economic" justification of layoffs, they define the amount of separation pay and advance notice required, they set out in detail procedures for prior negotiation with representatives of the employees and the modalities of recourse should a dispute arise, and they set out rules governing the use of short-term labor contracts. Thus, employment protection measures are pursuing at least three economic goals: to augment or preserve employment by diminishing job destruction, to reduce risk to wage-earners, and to incentivize firms to take the social value of jobs into account. The rest of this chapter will try to show that highly intrusive employment protection legislation attains none of these goals. We maintain, in addition, that the concept of social value underlying the last of these goals should serve as the basis for a different approach to the protection of employment.

Too much employment protection protects employment badly

Legislation making layoffs more difficult has an ambiguous effect on the volume of employment. It certainly cuts back on job destruction, but it also diminishes job creation, since firms fear being unable, in future, to destroy unprofitable jobs protected by the legislation. Employment protection is therefore favorable to employment if it reduces job destruction more than it reduces job creation. Theoretical analysis gets us this far and no farther. So assessment of the impact of employment protection remains primarily an empirical question. Much research has tackled this problem during the last decade.[2] As a general rule, it tries to show a correlation, positive or negative, between the "rigor" of employment protection and the rate of unemployment, taking care to bracket all the other forces that might affect unemployment and employment. The principal conclusions of this research are as follows:

• The rigor of employment protection has no significant effect on the rate of unemployment. Hence, more rigorous employment protection does not help to reduce the rate of unemployment.

• More rigorous employment protection increases the duration of unemployment.[3]

• More rigorous employment protection reduces the employment rate (that is, the proportion of persons of working age who are holding a job).[4]

It is mainly the employment rates of young people and people over 50 that are weaker in countries where employment protection is more rigorous. In sum, legislation making it harder for a firm to separate from an employee appears to be unfavorable to employment, in particular that of persons whose insertion into the labor market is harder anyway, such as young people, women, and older adults.

Employment protection protects badly against uncertainty

Employment protection stabilizes the income of certain wage-earners, but does so at the cost of greater uncertainty for others. In this respect, the contrast between the United States and France is striking. In the United States, layoffs represent around 40 percent of all exits from employment, while in France they reach 8 percent ("economic" layoffs account for less than 2 percent of exits from employment, even in years when the economy slumps). In the United States, quits represent around 54 percent of all exits from employment, while in France they reach 20 percent. Thus, the regulations governing economic layoffs directly affect only a very small proportion of exits from employment. Firms are essentially managing their personnel requirements by jockeying with short-term contracts (of fixed duration, generally 18 months). The terminations of these contracts represent around 53 percent of all exits from employment in France.

Employment protection *à la française* modifies the hiring and firing policies of firms without significantly influencing the number of jobs they need. Its essential impact in the end is to divide up the risk in a very unequal fashion. Current legislation protects the jobs of workers with a certain amount of seniority, but drives firms to make lavish use of short-term contracts. Thus it accentuates the *dualism* of the labor market between, on the one hand, protected workers who have access to stable jobs and, on the other, workers who are forced to accept short-term contracts and unemployed persons with little chance, on average, of finding a new job quickly. Employment protection increases the well-being of the workers it protects, but degrades the well-being of others. It thus helps to entrench inequality.[5]

Other routes are possible. In the case at hand, unemployment insurance proves better suited to sheltering workers against drastic fluctuations in their income, since it allows the genuine mutualization of risk. We will see below that it is preferable to view employment protection as one factor within the wider framework of the unemployment insurance system.

The private value and the social value of employment

Modern economies are subjected to a permanent flux of technological innovations and changes in the preferences of individuals, necessitating the disappearance of some jobs and the creation of others. We noted in chapter 1 that a huge number of jobs are destroyed and created every working day, and we have shown that this incessant process of job creation and destruction is the underlying cause of growth. When a job vanishes for these reasons, it is thus not a loss for the collectivity, although it generally is for the person who held that job. Legislation that prevented the destruction would by the same token have prevented a collective advantage from being realized. But conversely there are other reasons that weigh in favor of preserving certain jobs that firms might want to destroy. They spring from the difference between the *private* value and the *social* value of a job.

A worker is engaged by a firm to produce goods or services. This production represents the *private* value of the job and is split between a wage for the worker and profit for the firm. But in a modern economy, a firm and its workers are not insulated from the rest of the world, and the decisions they take affect the well-being of other persons who have nothing to do with the firm. This influence of the decisions of some persons on what happens to others who are extraneous to the taking of the decision is called an *externality*; pollution is a well-known example. The decision to destroy a job can have repercussions going well beyond the interests of the firm and the worker alone: it can thus be a source of externalities. In this case, the value of a job for the collectivity—its *social* value—does not coincide with its private value. The social value is measured by the sum of the private value plus the value of the externalities.

One important cause of the gap between the social value and the private value of a job lies in the overall conception of the fiscal system. The largest portion by far of receipts to the fisc comes from persons who hold jobs. Unemployed and inactive persons contribute very little to the financing of collective goods and transfers. It follows that there is a gap between the social and the private value of a job, measured by the loss of compulsory payroll taxes, and by extra costs in the form of social transfers that are triggered when someone moves from the status of wage-earner to that of unemployed or inactive person. In most OECD countries, this difference is considerable and justifies a form of employment protection.

The mode in which unemployment insurance and all forms of welfare are financed is another cause, perhaps more important than the previous one, of a divergence between the social and the private value of a job. In most industrialized countries, unemployment insurance is financed by a tax based on wages, which is paid in varying proportions by both employees and employers; it is one component of what are collectively called payroll taxes. Under an efficient system of unemployment insurance, an employer who lets an employee go would have to take into account the externality arising from the financing of the unemployment insurance benefit then paid to that worker by other wage-earners and other employers through their contributions to unemployment insurance. Under an efficient unemployment insurance system, the employer would also have to take into account the fact that the job she has destroyed will no longer contribute to financing the system. Absent such efficiency, every firm relies on all the other firms and wage-earners to pay the unemployment benefits of the workers it lets go. The social value of a job exceeds its private value by an amount equal to the cost for society of the laid-off person while he is unemployed. In neglecting the externalities occasioned by their behavior when they let someone go, firms are reckoning only the private cost to themselves, not the real cost of this separation to society. In situations in which this real cost exceeds the individual cost to the firm, firms will have a tendency to destroy too many jobs.

The distortions induced by compulsory payroll taxes are not the only reasons for a gap between the social value and the private value of employment. Unemployment exerts a negative effect on one's state of health, and it can increase criminality and undermine civic spirit. As well, persons who have jobs frequently redistribute a part of their material resources to their families and to those close to them. Hence, employment contributes to ameliorating the general state of health and reducing criminality; it forms part of a web of social bonds that ensure a certain redistribution of resources. All these factors should be taken into account in judging the collective advantage resulting from decisions about job destruction.

Absent a set of rules making it costly to fire, a firm that decides to separate from one of its employees takes into account only the private value of the job it is destroying; it estimates that this private value is too low to make the job worth keeping. But this layoff generates externalities such that the social value is higher than the private value. Thus, the firm makes a decision efficient from its own point of view, but which does not conform to the collective interest. The state must then intervene in order to realign the interest of the firm with that of the collectivity.

In the last analysis, a policy of protecting employment can be justified by the goal of achieving this realignment. In fact, this is its only possible economic justification.

Incentives rather than official review

One way to remedy the underassessment of the social value of jobs by firms is to "fiscalize" employment protection by integrating it into the financing of unemployment insurance and the welfare system. The principle underlying this fiscalization applies in many life situations where insurance is used. A reckless driver puts her own life in danger, and those of others too. Her attitude may cost society dearly in medical expenses alone. This is why automobile insurance premiums depend on the personal history of each driver, especially the number of accidents she has caused. The same principle can be applied to terminations of employment. A bonus-malus mechanism, by which firms pay in to unemployment insurance at rates that rise with the number of jobs they have terminated, makes it possible to limit inefficient destructions of jobs. It constitutes a form of job protection that incentivizes employers to take the costs they impose on unemployment insurance and the welfare system into account when they destroy jobs.

Such a bonus-malus mechanism exists in the United States, where charges associated with the payment of unemployment benefits are assigned to employers through "experience rating." Employers who initiate comparatively more job separations and thus increase the burden on the unemployment insurance system must pay higher unemployment insurance contributions than those who initiate fewer separations. A "natural experiment" carried out in the state of Washington sheds an interesting light on the effect of this mechanism of experience rating. In 1985 this state adopted the mechanism, while the neighboring states of Oregon and Idaho did not. It has been observed that employers in Washington have less tendency to fire their workers, while claim denials have increased.[6] The bonus-malus mechanism, like experience rating, compels firms to take at least partial account of the social value of jobs in their firing decisions. But a quite different arrangement is possible, in which the courts decide whether layoffs are justified in terms of the common good. This is how things are done in France.

As the industrial tribunal noted in the Michelin case, an "economic" layoff has to be justified by the need to keep the firm competitive, not to make it more so. But when judges try to make that distinction, they quickly lose their bearings. A reading of the decisions of the Court of Cassation, the highest appeal court, is instructive. We learn, for example, that a job which duplicates another is not necessarily superfluous; or that the need to safeguard competitiveness cannot be equated to the need to make "financial savings." All this is amusing, perhaps, but a fundamental question remains: Should there be an official review of the "economic" motive for the layoff at all? To answer "yes" is to assume that an independent authority has the capacity to assess the social value of a job, which is the only objective basis for keeping or destroying it. But the way in which the labor market actually functions makes such an assessment impossible. Technical innovations and mutations of every kind in the environment within which firms evolve require millions of shifts in employment every year, which an administrative authority is totally incapable of evaluating and anticipating.

To believe that some department of the government can objectively assess the social value of jobs amounts to believing that it is capable of coordinating these millions of shifts. This is a pure bureaucratic illusion, one too often cherished by some parliamentary deputies. The outcome of a large portion of these shifts is *structurally* uncertain, and thus baffles any kind of forecast, let alone any kind of planning. This is another reason why the fiscalization of employment protection is more efficient than any sort of official "economic" review of the motives for a layoff. Fiscalization is based on rules that provide an incentive in a transparent manner and that are not subject to the heterogeneity and arbitrariness of the criteria of judges and the talent of pleaders. It is immediately operational, whereas a procedure to officially review the economic motive for a layoff requires long delays, especially when litigation ensues. Moreover, official review of job terminations entails an increase in the cost of laying workers off without reducing the cost of labor. In this way, employment protection legislation reduces the profitability of firms. Fiscalizing employment protection eliminates this drawback to the extent that the taxes firms pay when they lay workers off flow back to them as bonuses for hiring or as reductions in payroll taxes. The logic of fiscalizing employment protection thus lies in taxing job destructions while subsidizing job creations by reducing the cost of labor. This is why the fiscalization of employment protection can be favorable to employment, whereas administrative control of layoffs hinders it.

For all these reasons, we ought to get rid of official "economic" review of layoffs and make use instead of a fiscal toolkit allowing us to bring into alignment, on average, the private and the social value of jobs.

Unemployment insurance and employment protection are essential tools for enhancing the security of working life. But they can never keep pace with an economy in constant mutation, which demands a ceaseless adaptation of the quality of its manpower. One of the main goals of public policy on employment, and of state intervention in the areas of education and professional training, is to ensure that manpower can adapt to change. The next two chapters will show that, in this regard, the road to hell is paved with good intentions.

7

Education Is Not a Miracle Cure

In many European countries, education is regarded as society's miracle cure. No matter what the problem, education is the solution. Whether it is primary, secondary, higher, vocational, or continuous, everyone concurs on its virtues and would like to see more of it. A consensus has formed around the idea of "lifelong education." This unanimity is based on apparently unchallengeable premises: the education system makes it possible to acquire knowledge of use in working life, develops capacities of abstraction and synthesis, favors intellectual growth, and in short, "produces" individuals prepared to accomplish the ever more complex tasks that a modern economy, faced with international competition, demands. From this perspective, effective vocational training to give persons whose competence has been overtaken by technical progress or international competition a second chance constitutes one of the essential components of the educational system.

In an economy in which jobs are being created and destroyed by the million every year, well-trained manpower makes it possible to adapt without too much strain to an environment in perpetual evolution. Hence, investment in education is indispensable. But that does not imply that it should be expanded continually and indiscriminately in every possible direction. To enhance knowledge is expensive, often extremely expensive. In order to know whether it is desirable to educate more or educate differently, it is imperative to know whether the outlays made on education do improve the lot of the beneficiaries and are useful to society as a whole. To put it bluntly, the private and public payoff of the various components of the education and training systems should be audited in order to eliminate those that have proved inefficient and favor the ones that work.

Recent advances in the methodology of evaluation arrive at results that clash with common sense: many investments in the educational and training systems do not pay off, for society or even for the putative beneficiaries. This finding runs directly counter to the credo that the best way to improve the economic and social integration of individuals is to systematically increase spending on the school system and on vocational training. Although the integration of the individual into economy and society is certainly facilitated by the knowledge imparted in the educational system, it is also facilitated, and maybe facilitated primarily, by the quality of one's competence in relationships and one's capacity to work out a coherent life project. These assets are not acquired solely in educational institutions, but are transmitted in large measure very early, in the family setting. Children who lack them soon encounter difficulty at school, and that is often a predictor of a chaotic life path, marked by numerous periods of unemployment and a very weak capacity to acquire knowledge through vocational training programs.

Recognition of the importance of the family setting and the preponderant role of early childhood calls into question the traditional concept of public intervention in the area of training and education. It leads to recommendations that shatter the consensus described above. More precisely, three main guidelines emerge: public support should be targeted, not fired from a scattergun; it should be directed primarily at young people, even the very young; and it should be deployed, in part, outside the school system.

The payoffs of education and the role of the state

Joan earns more than Paul because she stayed in school longer. This cause-and-effect relationship between the time spent getting educated and earnings lies at the core of the theory of "human capital" developed and popularized by Gary Becker. According to this 1992 Nobel laureate in economics, formal study, and training in general, can be likened to *investments* that accumulate to form a stock of professional or vocational competence, the awkwardly named "human capital." From this perspective, investments in education should translate into higher incomes for those who benefit from them. Countless studies have been and are being devoted to the evaluation of the financial advantage linked to education. Naturally their conclusions vary according to places, times, the characteristics of the persons concerned, and what they studied. At present it is estimated that on average one year of extra schooling increases one's income in a proportion that varies from 5 to 15 percent, which signifies that one must get from 5 to 14 extra years of study in order to double one's income.[1] So education is an investment that pays, but it is not a gold mine. Learning takes time; time spent studying is a loss in the sense that it could have been spent working. As well, studying does not come cheap. In all the OECD countries, on average, a year of primary school costs around $5,000 per child, a year of secondary schooling $7,000, and a year of tertiary education $8,000.[2]

In theory, the full cost of this educational investment could be charged to the beneficiary. In fact, the state invests massively in the cost of education in all developed countries. In France, public spending on education represented 5.8 percent of GDP in 2000, and in the United States 4.9 percent. Everywhere, public spending on education outstrips private spending, which represents 0.4 percent of GDP in France and 1.6 percent in the United States.[3] The intervention of the state in education is justified first of all by concern for equity and democratization. Many households would be unable to give their children a basic education if teaching were a private, paid service, when a year of primary schooling costs around $5,000 per pupil. Free schooling makes everyone's chances more nearly equal.

State intervention is also justified on grounds of economic efficiency. An entirely private education system, leaving decisions about education and training to be sorted out by the free play of competition, would probably lead to an undereducated society. The main reason public education is preferable is that education generates *externalities*. Readers will recall that an "externality" is a situation in which an agent benefits (or suffers) from decisions taken by other agents without the consequences of these decisions being "priced" in financial terms. The education of an individual generally entails benefits of this kind for those around him. Education improves socialization, which is measurable especially by lower rates of delinquency for better-educated persons.[4] The educational level of mothers exerts a positive effect on the health of their children, even in rich countries.[5] Moreover, the transmission of knowledge and skills simply through informal discussion or through observing others contributes to the social efficiency of education: a student's performance is generally influenced by the average performance of the other students in the same institution,[6] and similarly the productivity of every worker depends on the knowledge and skills of his colleagues.[7] As a general rule, an individual's training has social consequences that do not necessarily bear a market value. In this case, the social payoff from education is greater than the private one, and individual decisions would lead to too low a level of training.

Hence there are good reasons for the state to play a role in education. But it is far from proved that governments systematically do so in a judicious and effective manner, and that is why it is essential to evaluate the impact of public intervention: we need to form a judgment about where it is desirable, and what forms it should take where it is. Such an evaluation poses formidable (and often unsuspected) problems, which have partly been overcome during the last decade. The progress achieved in this field sheds fresh light on the consequences of educational policy.

How to evaluate public policies on employment?

To find out whether a measure to provide training improves the employment outlook of those who undergo it, the pertinent question is this: What would the career trajectories of the same persons have been if they had not had that training? Only a comparison between the trajectories of those who respectively did and did not undergo the measure in question can supply an objective indicator of its efficiency. Unfortunately, such a comparison is impossible, since no one in the real world can be in two places at once. If we know that Mr. Brown spent six months on a training course and found a job subsequently, we do not know what would have befallen him without that training course. True enough; but this is still the right way to come at the question of the efficiency of a measure, for although we do not know what would have happened to Brown without the course, we do nonetheless know, or know how to find out, what the outcome was for someone resembling him who did not take that course. Let us suppose that the course Brown took was open to all unemployed persons older than 25 without a high school diploma. Let us also suppose that we know of another unemployed person by the name of Green, older than 25 and without a diploma, who did not take the course in question. The usefulness of the course to Brown can be assessed by comparing his career trajectory to that of Green. If, six months or two years or five years after the course ended, we observe that Brown is holding a job while Green is still unemployed, can we state that the course was helpful to Brown? No, because it may be that Brown has certain characteristics (his professional background is stronger, he spent less time unemployed, he dresses better than Green, he speaks English more correctly, he fits in more easily with the other employees in the firm, he is more motivated or more intelligent, and so on) among which lie the real reasons for his success, without the course having had anything to do with it. This problem arises from the fact that entry into the course results from a selection—on the part of workers who apply for it, but also on the part of the authorities in charge, who generally have a limited number of places available. Thus, we cannot seriously evaluate the impact of a public program without confronting this "selectivity bias."

Awareness of this problem (a classic one in medical research) has made possible important advances in the evaluation of public policies.[8] The basic premise of these advances is that we take into account the largest possible quantity of information, captured in surveys, in order to compare the performances of individuals whose characteristics are as much alike as possible. With this premise in mind, the researchers construct two groups—one comprising persons who underwent the public policy measure in question (the test group), the other comprising persons who did not (the control group)—in such a way that each individual characteristic occurs with the same frequency within each group. For example, both groups must have the same percentage of women, the same percentage of persons without previous vocational experience, and so on. In practice, it is necessary to gather information on the trajectories of thousands, even tens of thousands, of unemployed persons older than 25 without high school diplomas. It is also necessary to gather as much information as possible on their individual characteristics. The researchers can then proceed to make a comparison between the average trajectories of the test group and of the control group, and thus formulate a finding about the average impact of the course on persons whose observable characteristics are similar.

But this finding still does not permit a judgment of the efficiency of the course, inasmuch as the researchers cannot rule out the possibility that those who took the course had particular characteristics, not captured by the surveys, that differentiated them from those who did not.[9] For example, the persons who took the course might have been more highly motivated and dynamic. In that case, if the researchers note that these persons subsequently find jobs more frequently than others with identical observable characteristics who did not take the course, they will be unable to determine whether that was caused by the course or by the particular nonobservable characteristics of those who took the course. One might think that there was a good chance of canceling out, or at least considerably reducing, the influence of unobservable characteristics if the list of observable characteristics is sufficiently long. Many studies show that this is generally not the case. Aware of the problem, statisticians have worked out methods for taking into account these selectivity biases.[10]

If in the end it is established that the average efficiency of the course is positive, that is evidently not the same as saying that the course helped everyone who took it. It simply means, and this is the essential thing, that on average the course improves the employment outlook of individuals: it might improve employment chances a lot for some and make them worse for others.

Public support for adult training

The great majority of evaluations of training programs that do take into account selectivity problems come from the United States.[11] European evaluations got started later and are still not numerous, although their number has grown significantly since the middle of the 1990s. From all this research it emerges that the only training programs that achieve a certain efficiency are those aimed at women older than 25 who come from underprivileged backgrounds. These programs are clearly less beneficial for adult males, and even frankly disappointing for young people, especially young men. It also emerges that it is the least skilled individuals who derive the least advantage from training programs. Since these programs are costly, their net payoff is very often negative, which means that it would doubtless be preferable to give the resources utilized directly to their beneficiaries, instead of making them enter programs that do not really improve their situation on the labor market, and that might even handicap them by creating a stigma.

From this perspective, the oft-proclaimed benefits of "ongoing training" are far from proved. At the outset, it was to counter the danger of underinvestment in training—this danger is real, as we have seen—that France set up a system in 1971 compelling firms to make outlays on training for their employees. As of 1 January 2004, firms with more than ten employees must spend 1.6 percent of their total wage bill on this outlay, and employers who do not spend that much must pay the difference to training organizations. Using data from a vast survey by INSEE (the French National Institute for Statistics and Economic Studies) on this topic, Dominique Goux and Éric Maurin found that the wage gain of an employee who received ongoing training appeared to be considerable at first sight: on the order of 5 percent for a *week* of training.[12] If that figure corresponds to a real relationship of cause and effect, then we should promote this type of training immediately and massively, since it clearly delivers a better return than the traditional education system, which improves wages in a range of 5 percent to 15 percent per *year* of school. Unhappily, the authors of the study go on to reveal that there was no miracle after all: the wage increment of workers who had vocational training comes solely from their personal characteristics. In other words, wage-earners who are judged the most productive for the firm are the ones who benefit from training courses and higher wage increases; the workers whose training already falls short practically never get it, since firms have an interest in targeting their training investment at employees who provide them with the greatest return (managers, technicians, employees who are already skilled). They also have an interest in putting their training investment into highly specialized trades and skills that, in the majority of cases, are not marketable outside the firm.

This explains why the beneficiaries of training stay with the firm for a long time, and the observed absence of any extra wage boost for those who do change employers after having received training (the number of whom, as it happens, is small).

The arrangements for ongoing training *à la française* are therefore not making a significant contribution to improving the abilities of workers with little training at the outset. The firms that do need to train their employees to execute specific tasks would have done so whether or not these arrangements were in place (such firms generally spend more than the compulsory minimum), and for all the others, the outlay on training either pays for courses that reward the best employees or becomes a "tax" paid to training organizations.[13] It is a well-intentioned mistake to believe that ongoing training for all, and better yet "lifelong training," are panaceas that will only yield greater benefits as the resources devoted to them are increased. In reality, the efficiency of this type of policy is not at all established, and the consensus surrounding it depends more on faith—all training is good *by its very essence*—than it does on objective scrutiny of the results. These strictures do not apply, however, to programs aimed at young children from underprivileged backgrounds.

Helping children and adolescents from underprivileged backgrounds

Aid targeted at young children from underprivileged backgrounds is distinctly more efficient than that for adults. The Perry Preschool Program, in existence in the state of Michigan since 1962, sets the standard in this area.[14] The goal of this program is to develop intellectual capacity and to favor socialization, focusing on children aged three and four. They are given preschool coaching and guidance for two and a half hours daily from Monday to Friday in small groups (one adult for six children), for two years. During this period, the staff have weekly meetings, an hour and a half long, with the parents, and the parents themselves meet in small groups every month.

The effect of the Perry Preschool Program has been evaluated in a controlled experiment involving 123 African-American children from underprivileged backgrounds with low IQs (between 70 and 85). Of these 123 children, 58 were enrolled in the program and 65 were assigned to a

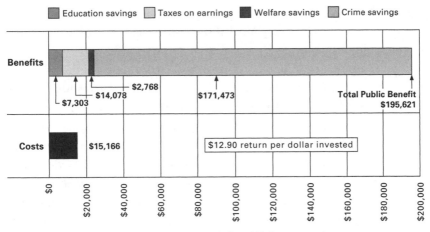

Figure 7.1
High/Scope Perry Preschool Program public costs and benefits. Source: www.highscope.org/Research/PerryProject/PerryAge40SumWeb.pdf.

control group that was not enrolled. The children who took part in the experiment were followed at regular intervals up to the age of 27. Figure 7.1 sums up the costs and benefits of the program, showing that it made a considerable difference to the degree of social integration and wage gains. Every dollar invested in this program returns $12.90 to the state in the form of savings on welfare ($0.18), future educational aid ($0.48), the justice system, the prison system, and damages to victims ($11.30), and of course in the form of extra tax income deriving from the improvement in the wages of the beneficiaries ($0.94). In addition to their positive impact on the well-being of the beneficiaries and the reduction of social inequality, the outlays on the Perry Preschool Program thus bring a strongly positive return to the budget of the state.

The success of the Perry Preschool Program is due to several ingredients which recur in all programs that have proved their efficiency. To start with, it is narrowly targeted and its budget is high: the annual cost per participant is more than three times higher than that of a child in primary school in France.[15] For another thing, the Perry Preschool Program helps children by involving their families. The participation of parents is one of the keys to the success of the program, and what is more, it has been found that parents whose children benefit from the Perry Preschool Program depend less on basic welfare and return to work with less difficulty.

Finally, although children enrolled in the Perry Preschool Program did not do better on tests of their IQ, they did obtain better results on tests of their noncognitive capacities like motivation and self-discipline. Hence, cognitive capacity is not always the decisive factor when it comes to social integration and successfully earning a living. In assessing education systems, we ought not to focus solely on acquired knowledge, as is often done, but also on other dimensions of personality that are at least as important for integration into society and in the labor market.[16] Acknowledging this also means recognizing that the school system cannot be expected to make up for all the deficiencies of society or to guarantee the future of every child.

From this perspective, the available assessments suggest that networks of mentors for children and adolescents have an important role to play. The association Big Brothers Big Sisters organizes mentorships for young Americans aged 10 to 16 belonging to single-parent families. Created at the start of the twentieth century, this association today brings together more than 500 local agencies across the whole United States, and supervises around 75,000 mentorships. The local agencies are financially autonomous, but must respect the criteria of organization and control of mentorships in order to belong to the Big Brothers Big Sisters network. These criteria essentially concern the selection of the young people and the mentors, the training of the mentors, and the frequency of the meetings between the youngsters and the mentors (the minimum requirement is three meetings of three to four hours every month for at least a year); and there are also meetings of the mentors, the children, and their parents. As a result of these requirements, the system has costs: $1,000 per child helped.

The effectiveness of Big Brothers Big Sisters was assessed in a controlled experiment carried out in the middle of the 1990s.[17] In the first phase, 1,138 children with the right profile for enrollment in the program were selected. Of these, 487 were drawn by lot to actually participate; they formed the test group. The others formed the control group, and were placed on a waiting list for a period of 18 months, which corresponds to the normal waiting period. Comparison of the behavior of the children in the test and control groups was done 18 months after the first meeting between child and tutor. It was found that drug use had fallen by 46 percent and alcohol consumption by 27 percent, and that the number of misdemeanors and rate of absenteeism from school were down significantly within the test group of beneficiaries (the "little brothers" and "little sisters"). A slight improvement in school achievement and family relationships was also observed. Evaluations of other similar programs reviewed by Pedro Carneiro and James Heckman come to similar conclusions.[18] Overall, measures consisting of helping children and adolescents to succeed in school through a system of mentorships framed by strict rules yield significant results, especially when they aim at young children from underprivileged backgrounds.

The reproduction of inequality

There exist critical periods of childhood development during which the principal pathways that govern the individual's ability to act and comprehend are laid down and can be modified. Motivation, the capacity to learn, and mastery of social relationships are acquired in the early years and condition the future prospects of children.[19] Experiments in neurobiology teach us that cerebral chemistry is influenced by the environment. For example, in humans exposed early to stressful situations, retardation in the development of the hippocampus—which forms a part of the brain involved in the consolidation of memory—has been observed, as have changes in neurotransmitters. The more anecdotal example of the learning of foreign languages illustrates this type of phenomenon in a striking manner: it has been established that it is practically impossible to pronounce certain sounds if these have not been heard, and uttered, before the age of six.[20] The particular pronunciation of the French language, lacking a tonic accent, causes French people to speak most foreign languages with an immediately recognizable accent, except for those who have had the opportunity to assimilate them in earliest youth. The acquisition of other personality traits more vital to social integration and success—for example, motivation, verbal aptitude, memory, mastery of social relationships, the capacity to learn and to take decisions—follows the same logic.

Much evidence points to the fact that the family setting profoundly determines the development of the capacities of children and adolescents, and so exerts a preponderant influence on their success at school and their future as adults.[21] The higher the income and educational level of their parents and grandparents, the less likely it is that children will have to repeat a year in primary school.[22] Yet financial constraints directly linked to the cost of primary education cannot be the cause of the poorer performance of children from underprivileged backgrounds. This schooling is free, and for modest families the cost is mostly borne by society. Financial constraints, like the educational level of the parents, act mainly on the quality of the child's environment *outside* the classroom—and this is likely the environment that matters most when it comes to success at school and social integration.

A study by Dominique Goux and Éric Maurin is very instructive in this regard.[23] They have found that 15-year-old adolescents who share their bedroom with at least one brother or sister—which is one adolescent in five—fail a year perceptibly more often than adolescents of the same age with their own rooms. Of course, the majority of adolescents sharing their rooms live in households with modest resources, and so the finding might simply mean that adolescents whose parents have low incomes do less well at school. Goux and Maurin nevertheless arrive at more telling conclusions by employing an astute strategy. In the first place, they find that the probability of sharing one's room is greater for adolescents whose parents have had children of the same sex. They go on to demonstrate that these adolescents fail a year more often than their peers whose parents have had children of different sexes. For the same income level, the lower rate of success at school of the adolescents whose parents have had children of the same sex can thus be entirely attributed to the more restricted living space at their disposal. More generally, living in cramped quarters exerts a significant impact on poor performance at school, and conversely success at school is intimately connected to the psychological comfort and good health of children.[24] The income of parents and their level of education are among the factors influencing this comfort. Social reproduction is to a large extent the result of what goes on in the family in early childhood and adolescence. The school system can also exert an influence in this respect, of course, but it is a mistake to expect too much of it.

The limits to intervention in primary and secondary schooling

Does it pay to reduce the number of pupils per class? More generally, should we be increasing the ratio of teachers to pupils everywhere, and spending more on primary and secondary schooling? Much research carried out in the 1990s in the United States (where primary and secondary schooling are supplied at public expense) yields the outline of an answer to these questions. The results of every study that undertakes this kind of assessment are highly controversial. Still, comparison of several hundred items of published work[25] points to the conclusion that outlay per pupil and class size have no real effect on the probability of pupils' staying in school longer or on their future incomes.[26] These results do not signify that the quality of classroom instruction has no influence on individual performance; rather, they signify that scattering resources piecemeal over the whole of primary and secondary education is not socially efficient.

Let us take the case of what in France are called "zones of priority education" (*zones d'éducation prioritaire*, or ZEP). Analysis of their impact suggests that the conclusions about public spending on education outlined in the previous paragraph for the United States apply to France as well. The purpose of these zones, created in 1982, is to channel extra resources toward geographic areas where there are particular problems, so as to offer schools there the chance to better adapt their pedagogy to local needs. The schools are selected on the basis of criteria such as the socio-professional makeup of resident families, the unemployment rate among parents, the presence of children of foreign origin, and the proportion of slow progress in learning. An institution classified as being in a priority zone benefits from an increase of around 10 percent in its resources per pupil. These extra resources are essentially used to reduce the number of pupils per teacher and to give bonuses (on the order of €1,000 per year) to teaching and administrative personnel. The education policies put in place in these priority zones muster substantial resources, and the least we should expect is that they prove useful. But it is far from certain that they do. A study conducted by Roland Bénabou, Francis Kramarz, and Corinne Prost on the ensemble of all these zones brings to light *no effect* of any significance on the success of the pupils (measured by the pass rate into the French equivalent of grade eight in the American system, and by the success rate in graduating from high school).[27]

These results should make us reflect, especially when set beside those obtained by Goux and Maurin in their study of the influence of living space on success at school.[28] On the one hand, it has been shown that the funds allocated to the priority zones have no effect on the educational outcomes of the children and adolescents there, and on the other it has been found that adolescents with siblings of the same sex, who are therefore more likely to have to share their bedrooms, fail a grade more often than do adolescents with siblings of a different sex. Putatively inconsequential circumstances like having siblings of the same sex can exert a large impact on outcomes at school, whereas large-scale pedagogical projects exert practically none. The results of these two studies underline the need to evaluate public interventions in education with care. Education is a field in which it is possible to spend a great deal with no apparent benefit to the populations supposedly implicated.

For Bénabou and his colleagues, the failure of the priority zones is largely attributable to a problem of targeting. Support programs should bring large resources to bear on a smaller number of institutions, following explicit and transparent criteria, instead of applying a more widespread, and necessarily less generous, policy. The authors emphasize as well that these interventions have to be evaluated using a "modern methodology, like that currently applied in the field of medicine (and more recently in sociology and education), including treated groups and control groups, random selection, and long-term follow-up of individuals." The record of the Job Corps established in the United States in 1964 illustrates and reinforces this conclusion.

The Job Corps is a program for young people aged 16 to 24 who are failing in school. Around 60,000 of them are enrolled every year in the program, which is a very costly one. The Job Corps offers courses, apprenticeships, and participation in a wide array of extracurricular activities intended to promote personal responsibility and self-discipline. The enrollees have to reside in the institutions offering these programs. Each youth stays in the program for around eight months at an average cost of $16,500 to the taxpayer. Comparison of this amount with the average annual outlay for a student in secondary school, which is around €7,000 in France (roughly equal to $7,000), indicates that the Job Corps does indeed not come cheap.

That it works was established in a controlled experiment carried out in the middle of the 1990s, which compared the performance of almost 7,000 young people who benefited from the program (the test group) with that of 4,500 others who wished to join but were not admitted (the control group).[29] The two groups were followed for four years after the test group left the program. Those who had been in the Job Corps had incomes 12 percent higher at the end of the fourth year. They had less delinquency, their arrest rate being 16 percent lower than that of the youths in the control group. These results tell us that well-targeted programs, adequately financed, can bring a marked improvement in the integration of young people with poor prospects. Of course the gains from such programs have to be weighed against their costs, and on this point the assessments diverge.[30] But the cost-benefit analysis of a program is only one factor to be considered. According to criteria made popular by John Rawls, a program can be adopted if it improves the condition of society's least-favored members, even if its cost measurably exceeds its benefits to society as a whole.[31] On this basis, evaluation of the Job Corps suggests that programs aimed at youth in difficulty are worthwhile.

All in all, assessments of public intervention in the field of education and training arrive at convergent results. Let us briefly review them. The returns on education (or as we economists say, "the returns *to* education") diminish with age for all categories of the population. In other words, the closer one approaches to the end of one's working life, the smaller the payoff from training. The efficiency of education is higher for very young children who have weak capacities for learning and socialization than it is for very young children with high capacities. But the virtues of extra education fall off rapidly for persons with weak capacities as they get older.

What we should do, then, is to concentrate educational assistance on *young children* from underprivileged backgrounds and ones whose capacities for assimilation are weak, whatever their background. But if it is to be efficient, this assistance must satisfy three conditions: it must be targeted at a fairly restricted population, it must not pinch pennies, and it must privilege projects that involve the family setting where possible. This does not mean that there is nothing to be done for the most underprivileged *adults*. Rather, the conclusion to be drawn is that training is not a form of assistance well suited to these persons. It is not socially efficient, and it does not bring significant extra gains for them. If we have a choice, it is better to underwrite the hiring of this category of worker by resorting, for example, to lowered payroll taxes or reductions in income tax. Learning costs a lot and does not always bring a high return. Systematically increasing public intervention in education, ongoing training, and retraining in new skills is thus not always the optimum policy choice. We will see in the next chapter that, to a certain extent, governments have taken on board this diagnosis, since their "employment policies" comprise an impressive kit of tools mixing job creation in the nonprofit sector with subsidies for private employment, sometimes adding periods of training to top things off. We will also see that the massive utilization of tools that are inefficient leads to the waste of millions of euros every year.

8

Evaluating Public Policies on Employment

Work Experience Placement (Sweden), Job Corps (United States), Contract of Return to Employment (France), Youth Training Scheme (United Kingdom), Temporary Wage Subsidy (Switzerland), Small Business Tax Credit (United States), Workplace Introduction (Sweden), New Jobs Tax Credit (United States), Solidarity Employment Contract (France), Job Start Allowance (United Kingdom), Relief Work (Sweden), Integration and Training Course for Employment (France), Work Opportunity Tax Credit (United States), Work of Utility to Society (France)

What is all this?

This jungle of labels designates programs to boost employment set up by the governments of various countries. Some have vanished, others are still in existence. All have (or had) as their goal the improvement of the "employability" of persons who were without work. This not very elegant but highly evocative term refers to all the factors capable of influencing the employment prospects of unemployed persons. Hence, all these programs try mainly to give them theoretical or practical training, impart or restore good work habits, and let them accumulate occupational experience.[1] To get an idea of what is going on, let's take a quick look at some of these programs.

Youth employment and training measures
In the United States, programs to help disadvantaged or unemployed youth are focused primarily on young people who leave school with no job to go to, and those who drop out of high school prematurely. The Job Corps program is an example. It is aimed at young people from

difficult urban neighborhoods, who are required to take training that gets them out of their normal environment. Job Corps centers are located in both rural and urban areas and provide training, education, a place to live, and a variety of other support services necessary to prepare students to become more responsible, productive, and employable. Unlike Job Corps, apprenticeship and other types of training are not, for the most part, aimed specifically at the young. An alternative to traditional classroom instruction, such on-the-job training programs give employers an incentive, by means of a subsidy, to furnish specific training to disadvantaged categories of workers. An on-the-job training placement generally lasts from 3 to 12 months, and at the end of that period the employer has the opportunity to hire the trainee on a permanent basis. According to the Nobel laureate James Heckman, in the United States these programs make it possible above all to insert, or reinsert, certain persons into a work environment, and there may be no real distinction between them and programs that simply subsidize hiring.[2]

In the United States, except for job search assistance, most of the policy measures that have followed one another since the beginning of the 1960s are "supply side" measures that aim to increase the human capital of the recipients. This approach is shared by the Manpower Development and Training Act (MDTA, 1962), the Comprehensive Employment and Training Act (CETA, 1973), the Job Training and Partnership Act (JPTA, 1983), and the Workforce Investment Act (WIA, 1998). So the JPTA and the WIA seek to promote on-the-job training, classroom training, and work experience.

Employment policy in the United Kingdom focuses on unskilled youth. The Youth Training Scheme set up in 1983 and continued in the 1990s as Youth Training provides periods of training, financed by the public authorities, for this category. Training policies addressed to broader categories of workers are in place as well, like the Training and Enterprise Councils set up in 1991, which are decentralized organizations charged with creating occupational training programs under the auspices of large local firms. With the creation of Job Centers in 1987, followed by the launch of the New Deal program, emphasis was also placed on measures to enhance job searching.

In France, the most important measures for youth are various forms of apprenticeship contracts, which can last from six months to three years. These contracts are aimed primarily at young people aged 16 to 25, and combine work experience with instruction given in a private-sector firm and at a training center. According to their age and seniority in the program, beneficiaries receive from 25 percent to 75 percent of minimum wage. In the area of vocational training aimed at long-term unemployed persons, the Integration and Training Course for Employment (*stage d'insertion et de formation à l'emploi*, or SIFE) is the main mechanism. It is reserved for unemployed persons over 26 and, in principle, for those experiencing the greatest difficulty (the long-term unemployed, welfare recipients, persons who are or have been subject to penal confinement, and so on). It offers training of variable duration in a workplace and/or in a specialized facility.

Subsidized employment

Subsidized employment covers a wide gamut of measures. Subsidies for employment in the private sector generally take the form of transfers to firms that hire members of particular groups. The transfer may be temporary or permanent, like the reduced payroll taxes for low-wage jobs in France, for example (see chapter 3). In the United States, the New Jobs Tax Credit, set up in 1977, was a very large-scale program of non-targeted subsidies for employment in the private sector. It was replaced at the beginning of the 1980s by the more limited Targeted Jobs Tax Credit and in 1996 by the Work Opportunity Tax Credit, which provides a tax credit for employers who hire certain targeted low-income groups, including vocational rehabilitation referrals, veterans, ex-felons, and food stamp recipients. Programs of this kind, which aim to increase labor demand, are the exception in the United States.

Public-service employment is addressed in principle to the young, the long-term unemployed, and economically disadvantaged groups. Its purpose is to allow persons in these categories to hold a temporary job in the public sector or in nonprofit organizations so that they can acquire work habits, minimal skills, or seniority, as a step toward finding a regular job (or simply to make them eligible for unemployment insurance). Programs of this kind form a large part of the spectrum of policy measures in Europe, but are practically nonexistent in the United States.[3]

In France, the Solidarity Employment Contract (*contrat emploi solidarité*, or CES), in existence between 1990 and 2005, exemplifies this approach. It provided for the employment of a person at or near minimum wage, for twenty hours per week for a maximum of two years, in public facilities, branches of local government, and nonprofit organizations. It was aimed at groups who were by definition having trouble on the labor market: the long-term unemployed, welfare recipients, recipients of the single-parent allowance, and so on. The state assumed the burden of at least 65 percent of the cost of the labor.

In a number of countries (including the United States and France), there also exist programs under which unemployed persons are given help in launching new enterprises. Most often this involves using unemployment benefits to subsidize unemployed persons willing to have a go at becoming self-employed. Observation tells us that in general this measure applies only to a limited number of unemployed persons.

The assessment of employment policy

Support for employment, whether public or private, costs a lot in some OECD countries. According to the OECD, this support amounted to 0.74 percent of GDP for the year 2003 in France. Comparable figures are 0.06 percent in the United States, 0.15 percent in the United Kingdom, 0.63 percent in Germany, and 1.01 percent in Denmark. Sweden spent only 0.52 percent of its GDP on support for employment in 2003, whereas in 1994 it spent 1.91 percent.[4] We will discover in what follows why Sweden cut its support for employment by almost three-quarters in the space of nine years. This expenditure also reaches a great many people in some countries. In 2003 the number of persons who entered employment policy programs represented 17 percent of the workforce in Austria, almost 9 percent in Finland, almost 8 percent in France . . . and 1.7 percent in Canada.

Considering the size of the outlay and the impressive number of beneficiaries in some countries, it is essential to find out what purpose is served by government aid to employment. One way to respond is to draw up the equivalent of a "body count," and measure success, as countries at war sometimes do, by the number of enemy bodies counted. In France, a large part of the civil service and many elected representatives adopt this perspective on employment policy. They take the view that every person placed in an employment support program should be counted as a victory in the battle against unemployment, or against poverty. Then all you need to know is the number of "passages through the measure," as French bureaucratic jargon has it, to have an indicator of the success of the measure in question. A good example is furnished by the report on the draft finance bill for the year 2003 written by a parliamentary deputy, Gilles Carrez. He sums up the achievements of the youth employment program for the year 2002 as follows: "At the end of the month of April 2002, 280,000 jobs had been created, and had led to 380,000 hires. Projects run by nonprofit organizations and local governments made possible more than 190,000 job creations and 257,000 hires. At the Ministry of National Education, 67,282 jobs were created and 96,198 hires realized. Within the national police, 20,000 positions have been created for activities in neighborhood security, and 26,368 young people recruited. As well, the Ministry of Justice created 2,000 positions and recruited 1,800 justice officers."[5]

This way of presenting the balance sheet of an employment policy measure by simply posting the number of its beneficiaries ought to be illegal: it deceptively conveys the idea that the efficiency of a measure is the same thing as the number of persons who undergo it. To be fair to our parliamentary deputies, they know that this is not the way to find out what the real bottom line of a measure is. The report on the evaluation of public policies presented to the National Assembly by deputy Didier Migaud in 1999 explicitly raised the question of efficiency. Appendix 3 in particular, dealing with "support for employment," advanced the idea that the most important thing was to find out what became of the beneficiaries when they left the program. Deputy Gérard Bapt, special rapporteur for this appendix, wrote, "it is first of all by following the trajectories of the returns to employment of the beneficiaries after they have left the programs supported that we must attempt to assess their *efficiency*."[6]

The problem is that, contrary to what the Migaud report states, you can follow up the beneficiaries of a program with all the care in the world and you will still have no indication of its efficiency. In all rigor, the question that has to be asked in judging the usefulness of a measure goes like this: What would have happened to the persons concerned in the absence of that measure? Establishing that 74 percent of the beneficiaries of a particular program are holding a job three years after leaving the program is not an answer to the question of the efficiency of that program. We pointed out in the previous chapter that information stated that way is generally misleading, and that correcting for the error sheds a quite different light on the effect of public policies for education and training. We will now see that the same is true for employment policy.

What the Swedish model has to teach us

Assessments of policy using adequate methodology[7] are current in the United States and are becoming more common in Europe. They have been systematically used to study the effects of the employment policies adopted in Sweden since 1990. Although this country has a long tradition of government aid to employment, the modern era of expansion in this field began at the end of the Second World War. At that time the goal of employment policy was to train workers to enable them to migrate from declining sectors toward expanding ones. Only gradually did it come to be seen as an instrument for combating unemployment. Then, in the early 1990s, doubts began to be raised about employment policy because it appeared powerless to stop unemployment from rising, despite being massively applied. At its apogee in 1994, expenditure on "active" labor market policies rose to 3 percent of GDP, and an evaluation of the return on that investment became necessary. Fortunately, Sweden had kept files on the outcomes of all unemployed persons since 1971. Since the middle of the 1990s, several dozen studies have exploited these files to try to assess the efficiency of employment support policies. A study carried out by Barbara Sianesi in 2002 is one of the most thorough of these, and her conclusions summarize the general tendency well.[8]

Sianesi focused on the efficiency of the six main programs in existence in 1994. She put together a sample of 30,800 individuals who entered into unemployment for the first time in 1994, and followed their trajectories on the labor market during the subsequent five years, until November 1999. Adhering to the general principles of policy evaluation outlined above, she compares the average trajectory of a person who benefited from a program in 1994 with the average trajectory the same person would have experienced if he had not taken part in this program. Some of these programs are aimed at the private sector, and others at the public and nonprofit sector. Private-sector help can take the form of hiring subsidies and training courses delivered on the job and/or in special facilities. Public-sector help includes programs to create non-permanent jobs, and others allowing for the temporary replacement of a permanent employee by a beneficiary of the program.

Sianesi finds that, compared to the average of the trajectories of persons who simply became unemployed and did not enter any program, the chances of finding a new "regular" job (a job unsubsidized by the government, in either sector) are appreciably *less*, over the whole five years of follow-up, for persons who got temporary jobs in the public sector and for those who took a training course outside a firm. This result may cause surprise, for what it means is that getting a temporary public-sector job or taking a training course outside a firm *reduces* one's chances, on average, of returning to normal employment. The likely explanation is that these programs do not increase the abilities of those who pass through them, and consequently send a bad signal to potential employers.[9]

Programs for on-the-job training and temporary public-sector job replacement come off better: they yield just about the same odds of returning to employment as simply being unemployed does! Subsidies to employment in the private sector, however, yield spectacular results. Compared to simply being unemployed, this measure raises one's chances of finding a new job by 40 percentage points practically from the moment one leaves the program, and throughout the whole five years the sample was followed.

Overall, subsidies to private employment clearly dominate all the other measures (a likelihood between 20 and 40 percentage points higher of landing a regular job). They are followed by temporary job replacements, which in turn dominate all the remaining measures. The reason in the latter case is that, because the beneficiary holds a job that permanently exists, she immediately finds herself in a real-world work setting which strengthens her abilities and her qualifications in the eyes of future employers. Ranking these employment support measures in terms of their efficiency gives us the following:

First   subsidies for employment in the private sector;

Second (shared)   simple unemployment, temporary job replacement, and on-the-job training;

Third (shared)   temporary public-sector jobs and training in special facilities.

Sianesi goes on to note that the ranking of the cost of these measures is practically the reverse. Per capita, the programs for training in special facilities and public-sector job creation are the ones that cost the state most dearly and are least efficient. Conversely, subsidies for employment, which in Sweden take the form of an abatement of around 50 percent of the cost of labor, are the least onerous for the fisc and the most helpful to the beneficiaries.

The exhaustive review of research on employment in Sweden carried out by Lars Calmfors, Anders Forslund, and Maria Henström reaches conclusions that coincide exactly with those of Barbara Sianesi.[10] They can be summed up this way: employment aid is more efficient, the closer the job being aided is to a regular job.

Confirmation of the conclusions of the Swedish experience

Michael Gerfin and Michael Lechner have carried out similar research on the employment policies in effect in Switzerland at the end of the 1990s.[11] Switzerland has the interesting distinction of having set up a large-scale program of "activation of passive spending" open to all unemployed persons. If they will accept a job paying a wage lower than the unemployment insurance benefit (which can be around 80 percent of one's last wage), then they receive the wage paid by the firm *plus* compensation from unemployment insurance which, taken together, amount to appreciably more than the unemployment benefit on its own. The extra compensation is paid for a year at most. During 1998, 20 percent of the unemployed held such a job at one time or another. No other employment support policy in Switzerland has a higher proportion of beneficiaries. Gerfin and Lechner find that this program increases the odds of returning to regular employment by around 10 percentage points, compared to simply being unemployed. All the other programs (training, temporary public-sector jobs, and so on) are *dominated* by simple unemployment. Compared to simply being unemployed, they *lower* the odds of returning to work, which confirms the conclusions of the research on Sweden. The program to activate passive spending works well: its beneficiaries move into "normal" jobs straightaway. They have retained good work habits, and they may have been able to improve their occupational skills. These things maintain or enhance employability, and so send a positive signal to potential future employers.

A study carried out on French programs aimed at low-skilled youth during the period 1986 to 1988 largely confirms this picture. By comparing, once again, a group of beneficiaries with a control group, it shows that measures promoting private-sector employment—particularly apprenticeship contracts—offer a better chance of returning to work than programs that focus on the temporary creation of public-sector jobs.[12] As we have seen, analysis of policy in Sweden arrives at the same findings: a spell holding a temporary job in the public sector does nothing to make one better prepared to hold a regular job.

What American studies tell us

In the United States the evaluation of labor market policies focuses primarily on the impact on wages. Table 8.1 illustrates, with several examples, the conclusions of social experiments regarding training programs carried out in the United States on groups of economically disadvantaged youth (men and women).

It turns out that the programs tested have high costs and do not really improve the situation of these young people, in terms of either employment or wages, except to a very modest degree for women. For young men, the wage gains are actually negative! Social experiments carried out in the United States also find that the least-skilled individuals are the ones who derive the least advantage from training programs. Temporary job

Table 8.1
The Results of Training Programs for Economically Disadvantaged Youth in the United States

Measure	Cost[1]	Employment growth[2]	Wage growth[3]
NSW	$9,314	0.3	−79
JOBSTART	$6,403	−0.9	−721
NJS (JTPA)			
Women	$1,116	—	133
Men	$1,731	—	−553

Notes: The programs tested are ones combining training and subsidy. JPTA = Job Training Partnership Act; NJS = National JTPA Study; NSW = National Supported Work demonstration.
[1] Marginal cost of treatment for one person for one year in 1997 dollars.
[2] Difference in employment rates between the treated group and the control group in the last quarter of the year subsequent to the experiment.
[3] Difference in annual average wages between the treated group and the control group in the first or second year subsequent to the experiment, in 1997 dollars.
Source: J. Heckman, R. Lalonde, and J. Smith, "The Economics and Econometrics of Active Labor Market Programs."

creation seems to benefit them, however. One possible interpretation of this result is that this type of measure gives persons in this category the chance to acquire work habits that more skilled categories already possess. The overall trend of other social experiments carried out on groups of economically disadvantaged women yields a somewhat brighter picture, showing wage gains that are relatively modest, although not negligible, and that are, moreover, persistent.

Overall, evaluations of training programs in the United States do not produce an impressive balance sheet in terms of their efficiency. Only the group of economically disadvantaged adult women appears to derive a real benefit for an acceptable cost from these programs. Conversely, the effects on other categories of the population, in particular young people, are most often very modest, and sometimes even negative.

From individual efficiency to social efficiency

To this point, we have dealt with the question of the efficiency of an employment policy measure by trying to quantify its net effect on its beneficiaries. This is indisputably the central question, since the purpose of a measure is precisely to affect the employability of those who undergo it. But in order to assess the *collective* or *social* efficiency of a measure, it is also necessary to know its effects on those persons who do not undergo it. If these indirect effects turn out to be strongly negative, then it might be time to think about doing away with the measure, even if it is giving some help to the beneficiaries. The indirect effects vary noticeably according to whether the measure applies to the public sector or the private sector. Let us start with the private sector, taking the example of the French program called the employment initiative contract (CIE). A contract of this type permits the firm to be heavily subsidized for the hiring of persons already facing long odds, for example, unemployed persons over 50. In the absence of this measure, some firms might have hired recent high school graduates instead. If that is the case in a significant number of firms, then the CIE is favoring the return to work of some of its beneficiaries (the "older" ones), while barring some others who are not beneficiaries (the "young" ones) from the labor market. Then the CIE will have caused young high school graduates to be *crowded out* of a job, as economists say, by unemployed persons over 50.

This crowding-out phenomenon may occur in other forms. It is possible that firms receiving employment aid may succeed in lowering their prices to the point of causing firms not being aided to fail. If so, the employment support will have increased hires in the firms being aided, while pushing workers in the firms not being aided onto the unemployment rolls. In order to gauge the extent of such crowding-out effects, surveys of firms being aided are regularly carried out, in France and elsewhere. In these surveys, firms being aided are asked what their intentions would have been in the absence of any form of employment support. As a general rule, the replies point toward the conclusion that substantial crowding-out effects do exist. But this is no more than an indicator, because for one thing it is hard to tell how much weight to give to a firm's answers to hypothetical questions about counterfactual situations, and for another (and more important) thing, these answers supply no indication about the crowding-out effects on firms not being aided.

These problems can be eliminated by using traditional econometric procedures that try to bring out eventual correlations between the amount of aid and the overall level of employment in a sector or a country; but the difficulties inherent in this type of procedure mean that their conclusions should be treated with caution. Nevertheless, Lars Calmfors, Anders Forslund, and Maria Henström have used such procedures to audit Sweden's employment policies: they find very strong crowding-out effects, stronger than those detected by surveys of top managers.[13] As things stand, the current state of empirical knowledge, while not supplying conclusive proof, does strengthen the case for the existence of sizeable crowding-out effects.

In the public and nonprofit sector, employment support measures can have slightly different effects. To start with, temporary jobs in this sector may crowd out permanent jobs. Another, and surely more important, consideration is that job creation in the public sector can exert a crowding-out effect on employment in the private sector. This might occur for fiscal reasons: a rise in public-sector employment generally necessitates an increase in fiscal pressure, and that might rebound by diminishing hires in the private sector.[14] The crowding-out effect might also make itself felt through a system of connecting vessels, like the parallel systems of private and public health care found in many countries. For example, if the state decides to increase the number of public hospitals, the number of private ones might fall, and there will be more nurses working in the public system and fewer in the private system. Public-sector jobs will have crowded out private ones. Such a crowding-out effect is possible in any area in which a role that might have been filled by the private sector is taken over by a public agency. On the other hand, in areas where public intervention appears to complement private-sector activity, public-sector job creation might stimulate private-sector employment. For example, better staffing of the public transportation system, with more ticket-takers and operators, might spur the development of private businesses. Increased public safety through the hiring of more police officers might favor the opening of new shops in troubled areas.[15] Only econometric research can shed light on the long-term influence of all these possible effects, by trying to pin down the nature of the correlations between the quantity of public-sector employment and the quantity of unemployment, or of employment in general. Though there are still not many studies of this kind, all of them do bring to light a crowding out (varying in size according to the study) of private-sector employment by employment in the public sector.[16]

Empirical research does yield (at least) one forceful conclusion: the closer the job being aided is to a regular job, the more efficient the employment aid. Conversely, it condemns outright, or argues for strongly trimming back, all programs to create temporary jobs in the public sector.

The priority in all countries should be to reinforce—or where they do not exist, to create—one or more independent bodies charged with evaluating existing programs using adequate methodology—the methodology of test groups and control groups exemplified throughout this book. All official reports, including parliamentary ones, ought to refer exclusively to such comparative assessments. It follows that every new program ought to stipulate which techniques will be used to evaluate it, including the collection and sifting of statistical data, and in some cases the setting up of pilot projects on a reduced scale permitting rigorous comparative analysis. Apart from that, the (likely) existence of substantial crowding-out effects is an invitation to be wary of massive programs with budgets larger than those of some government ministries.

9

Epilogue: Waiting for the Rain

Essentially, this book is a bearer of good news and bad news. The bad news is that the labor market does not function as we might wish it did. From one chapter to the next, we have seen that it is impossible constantly to raise the living standard of the greatest number without the system of production being continuously and profoundly reorganized; that it is not enough to increase wages or reduce the amount of time each person spends working to expand the number of jobs; that generous benefits for unemployed persons do not automatically guarantee a quick rehire—but neither do very stingy ones; that the retirement of the baby boomers threatens to aggravate underemployment; that massive public-sector job creation does not soak up unemployment; and even that taking a training course for several months does not significantly improve one's occupational outlook.

The good news is that today we have a little better idea than we did until not so long ago of what the best practices are in order to fight against unemployment and create jobs. These best practices are not always easy to apply, for they do not yield spectacular results in the short term, and inevitably arouse opposition, sometimes legitimate opposition, from vested interests. But building a new railway line presents the same difficulties: local residents are generally opposed, even if it is desirable for the common good. Whether it affects unemployment insurance, legislation on layoffs, the fiscal system, or the reorientation of employment policy, every public undertaking will bring disadvantage to some. The role of the politician is to overcome these difficulties so as to put in place best practices that increase the quantity of employment, and thus at one stroke the state's capacity to redistribute resources, especially in favor of the poorest. These best practices must satisfy a wide range of opinion, though differences will naturally persist. Economic analysis has tried to create a space of minimal consensus; let us briefly recapitulate its main features.

1. Ninety thousand jobs are destroyed and created every working day in the United States. This process is the motor of growth and material progress. If we want to improve our standard of living, we have to accept the fact that we live in a society where thousands of jobs are created and destroyed daily. A labor legislation based essentially on a logic of control and prohibition is ill adapted to reality; we should base our legislation on a logic of incentivization—which does not mean a complete absence of regulation. Employment should be protected through fiscal measures that give firms an incentive to assign more weight to the social value of jobs. Moreover, the unemployment insurance system should be grounded in a mutual commitment between the employment services and the unemployed person, in which adequate benefits and steady care and attention are furnished in exchange for meeting one's obligations and having one's efforts to find a job checked up on.

2. When the cost of labor at the level of minimum wage is a hindrance to employment, it is possible to remedy this by payroll tax relief, and even by subsidizing certain hires. This approach has the advantage of maintaining the purchasing power of the lowest-paid workers while not increasing wage inequality. But it is a costly tactic, because the reduced payroll taxes and the subsidies have to be underwritten. In general, making a small number of "the rich" pay up will not do the trick, so this solution demands a show of solidarity on the part of a very wide swath of households.

3. At first sight, withdrawing individuals from the workforce (for instance, through early retirements or exemptions from having to look for a job) and directly creating public-sector jobs appear to be the surest ways to reduce unemployment. Unhappily, the assessments we have show that we should be doing the exact opposite: reducing the size of the workforce destroys jobs, and in the long run, employment aid is more efficient when it is targeted at regular jobs in the private sector.

4. Public expenditure on vocational training may improve the chances of employment and higher income in quite particular circumstances. Very often its primary beneficiaries are those who have plenty of advantages already, whereas it has no effect on the most disadvantaged persons. In any case, training is not a miracle cure. Although the productivity of adult workers with few skills can certainly be improved, doing so is very costly, and it is generally more efficient to get these persons into work by reducing the cost of their labor. Public expenditure on training ought to be redirected in two ways: first, toward young children from disadvantaged backgrounds, with a focus on extracurricular structures and interaction with the family setting; and second, toward narrowly targeted programs with a long and costly follow-up of the beneficiaries, which is incompatible with the scattering of aid piecemeal over a large population.

These proposals are not necessarily designed to please, but they cannot be ignored. That they are so unfamiliar—or so unacceptable—not just to many citizens but also to many politicians, especially in continental Europe, explains in part why there is so much unemployment in this part of the world. One can understand why politicians, whether in power or hoping to get there, shy away from facing reality. Frequent elections encourage them to privilege the short term and give them an incentive to accommodate interest groups. But many public intellectuals bear their share of responsibility as well. By rejecting, often out of hand, the "bourgeois" or "liberal" (in the European sense) analysis of the market economy, they have deprived themselves of intellectual tools that would have enabled them to think objectively about the mechanisms that govern the production and distribution of wealth in the real world. This blindness means that many well-educated people today are still living in a world of economic thought that has more in common with phantasmagoric belief than with rationality. In such a world, we await the return of growth the way our ancestors awaited the return of the rain. Of course, instead of dancing at the full moon, we invoke other consensual gods in incantatory fashion (major European Union projects, lifelong training, etc.), but in reality all we are doing is telling ourselves that the rain will have to come sometime and keeping our fingers crossed that it happens before the next election rolls around.

To face up to reality and try to understand it, we need to escape from the realm of belief and advance resolutely into the world of evaluation and assessment, above all when it comes to public policy. In order to do so, we need to ensure that the assessments made are independent of the executive power responsible for the actual operation of policy on employment.

Institutional Acronyms and Websites

BLS   Bureau of Labor Statistics, U.S. Department of Labor; http://www.bls.gov

CEPR   Centre for Economic Policy Research (U.K.); http://www.cepr.org/

CREST   Centre de Recherche en Économie et Statistique (Center for Research in Economics and Statistics, France); http://www.crest.fr/Pageaccueil/index.html

IFAU   Institutet för Arbetsmarknadspolitisk Utvärdering (Institute for Labor Market Policy Evaluation, Sweden); www.ifau.se

INSEE   Institut National de la Statistique et des Études Économiques (National Institute for Statistics and Economic Studies, France); http://www.insee.fr/fr/home/home_page.asp

IZA   Institut zur Zukunft der Arbeit (Institute for the Study of Labor, Germany); http://www.iza.org/index_html

NBER   National Bureau of Economic Research (U.S.); http://www.nber.org/

OECD   Organization for Economic Cooperation and Development; http://www.oecd.org (for the Economics Department and its Working Papers, http://www.oecd.org/eco)

SIAW   Schweizerisches Institut für Aussenwirtschaft und Angewandte Wirtschaftsforschung (Swiss Institute for International Economics and Applied Economic Research); http://www.siaw.unisg.ch/

Notes

Introduction

1. These ideas are not entirely new. In *The Theory of Economic Development*, published in 1934, Joseph Schumpeter had emphasized the links between economic growth and the reorganization of the system of production. But it was only toward the end of the 1980s that advances in information technology made it possible to exploit millions of observations which revealed the extent of the processes of job creation and destruction, and their close relationship to growth.

Chapter 1

1. The evaluation of job destruction and creation raises tricky problems. The usual procedure is to use a sample of firms whose workforces have been observed at two precise dates (for example, 1 January and 31 December, thus a span of one full year). If, between these two dates, a firm increases its workforce, this increase is counted as so many jobs created. Conversely, if a firm reduces its workforce between the two dates, this reduction is counted as so many jobs destroyed. The rate of destruction is equal to the total number of destructions divided by the average stock of jobs of all the firms in the sample over the period. Using this method, we get an annual rate of job destruction on the order of 10 percent. For a sample of countries, including the United States, see the contribution by Steven Davis and John Haltiwanger, "Gross Job Flows," in Orley Ashenfelter and David Card, eds., *Handbook of Labor Economics*, vol. 3B (Amsterdam and New York: Elsevier Science, 1999), ch. 41, pp. 2711–2805; for France, see the article by Richard Duhautois, "Les réallocations d'emplois en France sont-elles en phase avec le cycle?" *Économie et statistique* 351 (2002). However, this method underestimates job creation and destruction, inasmuch as it neglects the destructions and creations resulting from short-term swings in activity. It also neglects modifications in the structure of employment within a firm, which can, for example, destroy workers' jobs and create management jobs without altering the size of its workforce. Research attempting to estimate such supplementary job destruction and creation suggests that both are substantial.

Taking them into account leads to an annual rate of destruction on the order of 15 percent; see our book *Labor Economics* (Cambridge: MIT Press, 2004), ch. 9. In the United States, as of November 2005, there are 142.6 million civilian jobs, which gives around 21.5 million jobs destroyed every year, or around 90,000 jobs destroyed per working day (on the basis of 240 working days in a year). In France there are 15.5 million jobs in the nonagricultural private sector, which gives around 2.3 million jobs destroyed every year, or around 10,000 jobs destroyed per working day. Note that for France these figures underestimate the total volume of movements of employment, since they exclude agriculture, non-profit organizations, and the public sector (comprising 8 million jobs), which also contribute to job destruction and creation.

2. See the study by Steven Davis, Jason Faberman, and John Haltiwanger, "The Flow Approach to Labor Markets: New Data Sources, Micro-Macro Links and the Recent Downturn," *IZA Discussion Paper* no. 1639 (2005), available at www.iza.org.

3. See in particular chapter 7 of Schumpeter's *Capitalism, Socialism, and Democracy*, 6th edition with a new introduction by Tom Bottomore (London and Boston: Unwin Paperbacks, 1987; first published in 1942).

4. Knowledge of these phenomena owes much to the work of the American scholars Steven Davis and John Haltiwanger; see in particular their "Gross Job Flows."

5. Viviane Forrester, *The Economic Horror* (Cambridge, U.K.: Polity Press, 1999), p. 46. First edition in French, 1996.

6. See Davis and Haltiwanger, "Gross Job Flows."

7. To be more precise, in a given firm or sector, the productivity of work is equal to the ratio of production, generally measured in dollars or euros, and the number of units of labor utilized. We speak of productivity per head if these units of labor are persons, and hourly productivity if the unit in question is hours.

8. For a study covering six OECD countries, see Stefano Scarpetta, Philip Hemmings, Thierry Tressel, and Jaejoon Woo, "The Role of Policy and Institutions for Productivity and Firm Dynamics: Evidence from Micro and Industry Data," *Working Paper* no. 329 (2002), OECD Economics Department; available at www.oecd.org/eco.

9. See Lucia Foster, John Haltiwanger, and C.-J. Krisan, "Aggregate Productivity Growth: Lessons from Microeconomic Evidence," in E. Dean, M. Harper, and C. Hulten, eds., *New Developments in Productivity Analysis* (Chicago: University of Chicago Press, 2001). This study also shows that in the subsector of automobile repair, productivity growth is entirely due to new firms in the subsector and that, on average, the older firms tend to have *lower* productivity.

10. See Lucia Foster, John Haltiwanger and C.-J. Krisan, "The Link between Aggregate and Micro Productivity Growth: Evidence from Retail Trade," *NBER Working Paper* no. 9120 (August 2002); available at http://www.nber.org/papers/w9120.

11. See especially Ricardo Caballero and Mohamad Hammour, "On the Timing and Efficiency of Creative Destruction," *Quarterly Journal of Economics* 111, no. 3 (1996): 805–852.

12. All these data can be found at the site www.eca-cokpit.com.

13. This remark and other information can be found in the article "Les compagnies à bas prix déferlent sur l'Europe," in *Le Monde*, 12 December 2002.

14. Eric Bartelsman, Stefano Scarpetta, and Fabiano Schivardi, "Comparative Analysis of Firm Demographics and Survival: Micro-level Evidence for the OECD Countries," research paper of the OECD economics department, no. 348 (2003), available at http://ideas.repec.org/p/oecd/oecdec/348.html.

15. See John Abowd, Patrick Corbel, and Francis Kramarz, "The Entry and Exit of Workers and the Growth of Employment," *Review of Economics and Statistics* 81, no. 2 (1999): 170–187.

16. For the International Labor Office, an unemployed person is a person of working age (15 or older) who meets the following three conditions: she is without a job, meaning she hasn't worked for even one hour during one reference week; she is available to start a job within a period of two weeks; and she has taken specific steps to look for a job during the four weeks preceding the reference week. The notions of "without a job," "availability," and "specific steps" can be interpreted in more or less restrictive ways, and thus lead to varying statistics on unemployment. The concrete problems posed by these interpretations and the procedures of international harmonization are discussed in the document entitled *Comparative Civilian Labor Force Statistics, 10 Countries, 1960–2004*, prepared by the Bureau of Labor Statistics (BLS) of the U.S. Department of Labor, Office of Productivity and Technology, 13 May 2005, available at www.bls.gov/fls/flslforc.pdf.

17. An American economist of Russian origin, Leontief was awarded the Nobel Prize for economics in 1973.

18. Stéphane Guimbert and François Lévy-Bruhl, "La situation de l'emploi en France face aux échanges internationaux," *Économie et prévision* 152–153 (January–March 2002): 189–206.

19. Evaluation of the consequences of the development of international trade on the labor market has given rise to many studies that adopt different methodologies, some of which differ from the balance of jobs approach. The latter is indeed an exercise in pure bookkeeping, and does not take into account price changes driven by the development of international trade. Our book *Labor Economics* offers a synthesis of the different approaches, the conclusion of which converges with that presented here.

20. Henry Farber and Kevin Hallock, "Have Employment Reductions Become Good News for Shareholders? The Effect of Job Loss Announcements on Stock Prices, 1970–1997," *NBER Working Paper* no. W795 (August 1999).

21. Sherrilyn Billger and Kevin Hallock, "Mass Layoffs and CEO Turnover," *Industrial Relations* 44, no. 3 (2005): 463–489.

22. John Haltiwanger and Milan Vodopivec, "Gross Worker and Job Flows in a Transition Economy: An Analysis of Estonia," working paper, University of Maryland (2000).

23. David Brown and John Earl, "Job Reallocation and Productivity Growth under Alternative Economic Systems and Policies: Evidence from the Soviet Transition," *Working Paper* no. 514 (2002), William Davidson Institute, University of Michigan; available at www.wdi.bus.umich.edu.

24. These mechanisms are brilliantly described by Joseph Schumpeter in *Capitalism, Socialism, and Democracy*. Philippe Aghion and Peter Howitt's *Endogenous Growth Theory* (Cambridge: MIT Press, 1998) presents the modern developments of the Schumpeterian approach, to which these two authors have largely contributed.

25. Jean-Claude Michéa maintains in a coherent fashion that "progressive" ideology, common to all parties or movements that identify as belonging to the left, leads inevitably to the acceptance of liberalism. According to this philosopher, the first task of an "authentic" left must be to question the dogma of progress. See his book *Impasse Adam Smith: Brèves remarques sur l'impossibilité de dépasser le capitalisme sur sa gauche* (Paris: Éditions Climats, 2002).

26. An unregulated market economy may have many other drawbacks, in particular in its effects on the environment and the well-being of future generations. John McMillan, in *Reinventing the Bazaar* (New York: Norton, 2002), draws up a comprehensive balance of the advantages and drawbacks of this mode of organizing exchange.

27. These well-known facts are presented in works of economic history. See especially Karl Polanyi, *The Great Transformation: The Political and Economic Origins of Our Time*, foreword by Joseph E. Stiglitz, introduction by Fred Block (Boston: Beacon Press, 2001; first published in 1944); and Paul Bairoch, *Victoires et déboires: Histoire économique et sociale du monde du XVIᵉ siècle à nos jours* (Paris: Gallimard, 1997), 3 vols.

28. Amartya Sen, *Development as Freedom* (New York: Alfred A. Knopf, 1999), p. 112.

29. Marx's position on recognizing the market as a vector of freedom nevertheless remains ambiguous. See the discussion in Jon Elster, *Making Sense of Marx* (Cambridge: Cambridge University Press, 1985), pp. 204 ff.

30. See Monique Canto-Sperber and Nadia Urbinati, eds., *Le socialisme libéral: Une anthologie: Europe-États-Unis* (Paris: Esprit, 2003), which presents a collection of texts from a socialist-liberal tradition with ramifications in France, Germany, Italy, the United Kingdom, and the United States. According to the editors, "liberal socialism aims to return to liberalism as a political method of emancipation, and to show that socialism is, in its primary inspiration, a philosophy of freedom." [Translator's note: This anthology has not been published in English. But I will take the liberty of mentioning two books edited by Nadia Urbinati, who has also written important introductions to each, and translated

from Italian into English by me. The first is by a socialist who turned to liberalism, the second by a liberal who challenged fascism and statism: Carlo Rosselli, *Liberal Socialism*, edited by Nadia Urbinati, translated by William McCuaig (Princeton: Princeton University Press, 1994); Piero Gobetti, *On Liberal Revolution*, edited and with an introduction by Nadia Urbinati, translated by William McCuaig, foreword by Norberto Bobbio (New Haven: Yale University Press, 2000).]

31. The pragmatic school in philosophy defends a reformist position of this kind. On this, readers may consult the article by Daniel Brunson, "Richard Rorty, Philosopher of Liberalism? Notes on the Political Viability of Pragmatism," presented at the colloquium Pragmatism in the twenty-first Century (April 2003), available at http://www.newschool.edu/gf/phil/conf_spring03.htm. See in addition John Dewey's article "The Future of Liberalism," in *The Later Works, 1925–1953*, vol. 2: *1935–1937*, ed. Jo Ann Boydston (Carbondale and Edwardsville: Southern Illinois University Press, 1988), pp. 269–299. In this article Dewey, one of the principal founders of the pragmatic school in philosophy, develops a critique of the liberalism that places exclusive emphasis on private property and free exchange. He underlines its theoretical bent, which leads to to a stripped-down conception of society, and its incapacity to grasp historical relativity. Dewey defends a form of liberalism that challenges laisser-faire; this form of liberalism, based on the study of actually existing conditions, seeks to ameliorate the conditions of life by accommodating the defense of individual liberty. It also leads to foregrounding the fundamental importance of making assessments of the policies that are tried, the impact of which cannot be known a priori. We shall return to these themes throughout this book.

Chapter 2

1. Alfred Sauvy was appointed Secretary-General for Family and Population by General de Gaulle in April 1945, and was the director of the National Institute for Demographic Studies from 1945 to 1962. In *La machine et le chômage* (Paris: Dunod, 1980), he also tells of how the arrival of 20,000 Vietnamese refugees in France in 1977 let loose the same phantasms (p. 226). The National Employment Agency (ANPE) stated that there was no point in their making the least effort to find work, since there were already more than a million unemployed persons in France.

2. For example, Jean Boissonnat, in the preface to his new book *La fin du chômage* (Paris: Calmann-Levy, 2001), asserts: "The fall in natality and the lowering of the age of retirement, together with the economic upturn, are now creating a novel state of affairs: for the first time, the number of persons of working age is ceasing to rise, and will begin to decline starting in 2010. If growth is maintained, it is possible to foresee that France will soon have an unemployment rate of around 5 percent of the working population. All the discourses of the political class must be re-thought in light of this incontrovertible fact."

3. Many of the speeches of Fidel Castro are available in English translation on the site http://lanic.utexas.edu.

4. The site http://www.cuban-exile.com provides thorough documentation on the Mariel boatlift.

5. Fidel Castro was clever enough to mix individuals with particularly serious psychiatric or criminal histories in with the refugees. The crime rate in Miami did rise by 50 percent between 1979 and 1980, and on 17 May 1980 riots linked to the presence of the refugees led to 13 deaths. More than 2,700 Cuban refugees were repatriated to Havana for reasons having to do with their criminal pasts.

6. See David Card, "The Impact of the Mariel Boatlift on the Miami Labor Market," *Industrial and Labor Relations Review* 43 (1990): 245–257.

7. The relevance of David Card's conclusions rests on the quality of his choice of control cities, which needed to be as much like Miami as possible, so there will always be a margin of uncertainty. Absolute truth is not to be found in economics, any more than it is in any other scientific discipline.

8. See the article by David Card and John DiNardo, "Do Immigrant Inflows Lead to Native Outflows?" in *American Economic Review, Papers and Proceedings* 90 (2000): 361–367. See also George Borjas, "The Labor Demand Curve Is Downward Sloping: Re-examining the Impact of Immigration on the Labor Market," *Quarterly Journal of Economics* 118 (2003): 1135–1174. The paper by Christian Dustmann, Tim Hatton, and Ian Preston, "The Labour Market Effects of Immigration," *Economic Journal* 115 (2005): F297–F299, provides a synthesis of this issue.

9. In order to simplify, we leave out of this line of reasoning the fact that the productivity of a worker depends potentially on the capacities of other workers. More elaborate analysis would incorporate the interactions among the productivities of the different categories of worker. One would then take into account the possibilities of substitution among the different types of labor and capital, which would require resort to mathematical formalization to arrive at clear results. On this, the interested reader may consult the article by George Borjas, "The Economic Analysis of Immigration," in Orley Ashenfelter and David Card, eds., *Handbook of Labor Economics*, vol. 3A (1999), ch. 28, pp. 1697–1760.

10. It is the difference in the endowment of capital among the different countries of the world that is the root cause of economic migration. The abilities of every individual are evidently the same, wherever he finds himself. But the volume of "capital" with which these abilities must mesh is very different. The countries of the north, richly endowed with means of production and collective infrastructures, can offer the least-skilled workers better-paying jobs than the countries of the south can. An unskilled Chinese worker can multiply her wage fifty times by coming to work in France. In economic terms, limits on the intake of immigrants are linked to the impossibility of rapidly expanding the existing volume of capital (especially infrastructure). On all these points, see the article by Richard Freeman and Remcom Oostendorp, "Wages around the World: Pay

across Occupations and Countries," *NBER Working Paper* no. 8058 (2000), available at www.nber.org.

11. Jennifer Hunt, "The Impact of the 1962 Repatriates from Algeria on the French Labor Market," *Industrial and Labor Relations Review* 45 (1992): 556–572.

12. The working-age population comprises persons who are between 15 and 64 years of age.

13. Joshua Angrist and Adriana Kugler, "Productive or Counter-Productive? Labor Market Institutions and the Effect of Immigration on European Union Natives," *IZA Discussion Paper* no. 433 (2002), available at http://www.iza.org, and published in *Economic Journal* 113 (2003): F302–F331.

14. Jean-Marc Burniaux, Romain Duval and Florence Jaumotte, "Coping with Ageing: A Dynamic Approach to Quantify the Impact of Alternative Policy Options on Future Labour Supply in OECD Countries," *OECD Economic Department Working Paper* no. 371 (2003); available at www.oecd.org.

15. See Burniaux, Duval and Jaumotte, "Coping with Ageing."

16. See Paul Bairoch, *Victoires et déboires: Histoire économique et sociale du monde du XVIe siècle à nos jours*.

17. See the fine work edited by Alain Corbin, *L'avènement des loisirs* (Paris: Aubier, 1995).

18. Cited in the report of the General Commissariat of the Plan, *Réduction du temps du travail: Les enseignements de l'observation*, report of the commission headed by Henri Rouilleault (Paris: Documentation française, 2001), p. 74.

19. Note that in such a world, employment would increase to the degree that workers were less efficient, given that employers supposedly hire the number of persons they need to attain their production targets. If that were so, a simple remedy for unemployment would be to force employees to work more slowly and less efficiently, so that new employees could be hired.

20. The lowered payroll charges for low-wage jobs represent 1.3 percent of GDP, of which 0.7 percent corresponds to the reductions provided for within the framework of the Aubry laws.

21. See the work of Gilbert Cette and Dominique Taddei, *Réduire la durée du travail* (Paris: Le Livre de Poche, 1997; series "Réferences").

22. Here we refer to studies based on survey data analyzing the impact of reductions in time worked that are not financed by lowered payroll charges. Much research has been devoted to the impact of reduced work time, utilizing various methods of constructing model simulations. Other research has studied the impact of incentive measures that simultaneously reduce payroll charges and time worked. This research is summarized in Pierre Cahuc and Pierre Granier, eds., *La réduction du temps de travail: Une solution pour l'emploi?* (Paris: Economica, 1997); Pierre Cahuc, "Les expériences françaises de réduction du temps de travail: Moins d'emplois et plus d'inégalités," *Revue française d'économie* 15,

no. 3 (January 2001): 141–166; the report of the General Commissariat of the Plan, *Réduction du temps du travail*; and the book by François Contensou and Radu Vranceanu, *Working Time: Theory and Policy Implications* (Cheltenham, UK: Edward Elgar Publishing, 2000).

23. Jennifer Hunt, "Has Work-Sharing Worked in Germany?," *Quarterly Journal of Economics* 114 (1999): 117–148.

24. Bruno Crépon and Francis Kramarz, "Employed 40 Hours or Not-Employed 39: Lessons from the 1982 Workweek Reduction in France," *Journal of Political Economy* 110 (2002): 1355–1389.

Chapter 3

1. The complete text of Chirac's speech is available at http://notre.republique. free.fr/CHIRAC95pdt.htm. The beginning of the passage quoted alludes to a plan commission presided over by Alain Minc, which was tasked with reporting to the prime minister at the time, Édouard Balladur, on "the challenges of the year 2000." In the part of this report dedicated to wage policy, the commission had put forward the idea that in a phase of economic recovery, "wage costs per head . . . should increase less quickly than productivity, so that the surplus accruing from the growth may be allocated first to job creation." In plain language, this meant that wage rises might hinder job creation. The report written by Alain Minc was published in 1994 under the title *La France de l'an 2000* (Paris: Odile Jacob, 1994).

2. David Card and Alan Krueger, "Minimum Wages and Employment: A Case Study of the Fast-Food Industry in New Jersey and Pennsylvania," *American Economic Review* 84 (1994): 772–793. See as well their book *Myth and Measurement: The New Economics of the Minimum Wage* (Princeton: Princeton University Press, 1995).

3. See David Neumark and William Wascher, "Minimum Wages and Employment: A Case Study of the Fast-Food Industry in New Jersey and Pennsylvania: Comment," *American Economic Review* 90 (2000): 1363–1393; and the reply of David Card and Alan Krueger, "Minimum Wages and Employment: A Case Study of the Fast-Food Industry in New Jersey and Pennsylvania: Reply," *American Economic Review* 90 (2000): 1397–1420.

4. Cf. Card and Krueger, *Myth and Measurement*, ch. 3.

5. Card and Krueger, *Myth and Measurement*, ch. 2 and 4.

6. George Stigler, "The Economics of Minimum Wage Legislation," *American Economic Review* 36 (1946): 358–365; the quoted passage at p. 360. Stigler received the Nobel Prize for economics in 1982 for his original studies on industrial structure, the functioning of markets, and the causes and effects of public regulation.

7. For the sake of brevity in this theoretical section, we use "wage" to mean the "cost of labor," that is, the wage plus all the payroll taxes attached to manpower.

8. "Monopsony" means a single buyer. The employer disposes of monopsony power vis-à-vis the employee to the extent that the latter generally cannot get other employers to compete for his services in order to extract wage increases. This insight has stimulated a large quantity of research during the last decade on wage formation and the impact of wages on employment. Readers may consult two recent works on the subject: Alan Manning, *Monopsony in Motion: Imperfect Competition in Labor Markets* (Princeton: Princeton University Press, 2003); and Dale Mortensen, *Wage Dispersion: Why Are Similar People Paid Differently?* (Cambridge: MIT Press, 2003).

9. At the end of 2005, the federal minimum hourly wage in the United States is $5.15. There are numerous exceptions, including ones for young people under 20, students, and employees of small businesses; and the payroll taxes on employers amount to 7.5 percent of the wage. Fifteen states impose a minimum wage higher than the federal one, and two states impose a minimum wage lower than the federal one, the average being $6.62 and the highest being $7.35. The average hourly cost of labor at the level of minimum wage is thus on the order of $6 for the whole United States (for more information, go to the site www.bls.gov). In France, the gross hourly minimum wage is €8.03, with an average rate of payroll tax on employers on the order of 25 percent, markedly less than the full rate of 45 percent thanks to payroll tax relief on low wages. If we assume an exchange rate of €1 = $1.2, we get a cost of labor in France of $12.045, which is about 100 percent higher than the average American labor cost of $6.

10. See John Abowd, Francis Kramarz, David Margolis, and Thomas Philippon, "The Tail of Two Countries: Minimum Wage and Employment in France and the United States," *IZA Discussion Paper* no. 203 (2000); available at www.iza.org.

11. We may add one last argument to this diagnosis. In France the cost of labor at minimum wage (SMIC) did not always rise between 1990 and 1998. Policies of payroll tax relief even caused the cost of labor to fall in the periods 1993–1994 and 1995–1996. The *IZA Discussion Paper* of John Abowd and his colleagues highlights the fact that minimum-wage earners saw their chances of keeping their jobs *increase* during the periods 1993–1994 and 1995–1996, compared to those of workers earning slightly more than the minimum wage. On the other hand, it also points out that reductions in the cost of labor observed in the United States have had no significant impact on the chances of losing or keeping their jobs for minimum-wage earners.

12. Bruno Crépon and Rosenn Desplatz, "Une nouvelle évaluation des effets des allègements de charges sociales sur les bas salaires," *Économie et statistique* 348 (2001): 1–24. This article describes the method utilized and details all the results. The same issue of *Économie et statistique* contains comments clarifying the scope of this study. An English version of the article, entitled "Evaluating the Effects of Payroll Tax Subsidies for Low-Wage Workers," is available at www.crest.fr/pageperso/dr/crepon/crepon_angl.htm.

13. More precisely, they find that this payroll tax relief created between 255,000 and 670,000 jobs. The figure of 460,000 is thus an average.

Chapter 4

1. This natural experiment is analyzed in detail by Bruce Meyer, Kip Viscusi, and David Durbin in their article "Workers' Compensation and Injury Duration: Evidence from a Natural Experiment," *American Economic Review* 85 (June 1995): 322–340.

2. See Thomas Piketty, "L'impact des incitations financières au travail sur les comportements individuels: Une estimation pour le cas français," *Économie et prévision* 132–133 (January–March 1998): 1–36.

3. If, on the other hand, the goal sought was to combat unemployment by reducing the size of the labor force, this policy was doubtless ineffective, for reasons pointed out in chapter 2. Moreover, by taking women out of the labor market, the parental education allowance helps to marginalize them. Assistance in paying for the cost of childcare offers the advantage, from this perspective, of allowing women to participate in the labor market.

4. Strictly speaking, one ought to distinguish the "inactivity trap" from the "unemployment trap." The "inactivity trap" refers to persons no longer participating in the labor market, and therefore making no effort to look for a job. The "unemployment trap" refers to the case of certain job seekers who are looking for work, but who refuse to work for very low wages because of the amount of unemployment insurance or welfare they are getting. In practice, the boundary between these two types of "trap" is fuzzy. In order to simplify, we use the term "inactivity trap" to refer to both cases.

5. Denis Anne and Yannick L'Horty, "Transferts sociaux locaux et retour à l'emploi," *Économie et statistique* 357–358 (2002): 49–71. This article follows a long series of studies that have demonstrated the existence of inactivity traps in France. See in particular Guy Laroque and Bernard Salanié, "Labor Market Institutions and Employment in France," *Journal of Applied Econometrics* 17, no. 1 (2002): 25–48.

6. In France, the legal duration of a full-time job is 35 hours of work per week.

7. A description of this experiment and all the results can be found in the final report, entitled *Making Work Pay: Final Report on the Self-Sufficiency Project for Long Term Welfare Recipients*, edited by Charles Michalopoulos and published in July 2002 by the Social Research and Demonstration Corporation, Canada. This report is available at www.srdc.org/english/publications/SSP54.htm.

8. See J. Greenwood and J.-P. Voyer, "Experimental Evidence on the Use of Earnings Supplements as a Strategy to 'Make Work Pay,'" *OECD Economic Studies* 31 (2000): 52–79.

9. See Charles Michalopoulos, Philipp Robin, and David Card, "When Financial Incentives Pay for Themselves: Evidence from a Randomized Social Experiment for Welfare Recipients," *Journal of Public Economics* 89 (2005): 5–29.

10. The Self-Sufficiency Project is not the only controlled experiment that has tried to test the effects of financial incentives to return to work. Most of the other similar experiments have been done in the United States, and their conclusions converge on those of the Self-Sufficiency Project. For an overview, see Rebecca Blank, "Evaluating Welfare Reform in the United States," *Journal of Economic Literature* 40, no. 4 (December 2002): 1105–1166.

11. For a detailed account of the features of the EITC, see Blank, "Evaluating Welfare Reform in the United States."

12. For more details, see Richard Blundell, "Welfare Reform for Low Income Workers," *Oxford Economic Papers* 53, no. 2 (2001): 189–214.

13. See Richard Blundell, Mike Brewer, and Andrew Shephard, "Evaluating the Labour Market Impact of Working Families' Tax Credit Using Difference-in-Differences," report of the Institute for Fiscal Studies (2005), available at www.hmrc.gov.uk/research/ifs-did.pdf.

14. See David Ellwood, "Anti-poverty Policy for Families in the Next Century: From Welfare to Work and Worries," *Journal of Economic Perspectives* 14, no. 1 (winter 2000): 187–198.

15. For more detail, see Pierre Cahuc, "À quoi sert la prime pour l'emploi?" *Revue française d'économie* 16 (January 2002): 3–61.

16. Even if the assistance furnished by the WFTC can be reduced by two-thirds by reductions in other kinds of welfare payment, which is not the case for the premium for employment, the British system of negative income tax remains markedly more generous than the one used in France.

17. These studies were initiated by Lawrence Lindsey in "Individual Taxpayer Response to Tax Cuts 1982–1984, with Implications for the Revenue Maximizing Tax Rate," *Journal of Public Economics* 33 (1987): 173–206; and see especially Martin Feldstein, "The Effect of Marginal Tax Rates on Taxable Income: A Panel Study of the 1986 Tax Reform Act," *Journal of Political Economy* 103 (1995): 551–572.

18. Jon Gruber and Emmanuel Saez, "The Elasticity of Taxable Income: Evidence and Implications," *Journal of Public Economics* 84 (2002): 1–32.

19. This result applies at the threshold of a marginal tax rate higher than 63 percent. Gruber and Saez estimate "the elasticity of taxable income," e, using an equation of the type $ln(y) = eln\,(1 - t)$, where y designates the taxable income and t the marginal tax rate. The extra tax take produced by an increase in t is equal to $ydt + tdy$. Since the definition of e implies that $dy = -eydt/(1 - t)$, the increase in tax take is equal to $ydt - (teydt/(1 - t))$. This increase is annulled for a marginal rate equal to $1/(1 + e)$. Gruber and Saez obtain a value of e on the order of 0.6 for incomes greater than \$100,000.

20. Thomas Piketty, "Les hauts revenus face aux modifications des taux marginaux supérieurs de l'impôt sur le revenu en France, 1970–1996," *Économie et prévision* 138–139 (1999): 25–60.

21. Piketty finds an elasticity of taxable income on the order of 0.2 for high incomes.

22. Readers will find more detail on this matter in Thomas Piketty, "Income Inequality in France, 1901–1998," *Journal of Political Economy* 111, no. 5 (2003): 1004–1042.

23. See the article by Herwig Immervoll, Henrik Kleven, Claus Kreiner, and Emmanuel Saez, "Welfare Reform in European Countries: A Micro Simulation Analysis," forthcoming in *Economic Journal*.

Chapter 5

1. See chapter 1.

2. According to the Bureau of Labor Statistics, the job openings rate (equal to the number of job openings divided by employment plus job openings) in the nonfarm sector amounted to 2.5 percent in January 2005.

3. Jean-Louis Zanda, "Les employeurs qui rencontrent des difficultés pour embaucher," *Les Cahiers de l'observatoire de l'ANPE* (March 2001): 27–52.

4. See Daron Acemoglu and Robert Shimer, "Productivity Gains from Unemployment Insurance," *European Economic Review* 44 (2000): 1115–1125.

5. In the great majority of industrialized countries, unemployment insurance pays benefits for a limited time, after which the unemployed become clients of a welfare system, which pays them a smaller allowance.

6. Brigitte Dormont, Denis Fougère, and Ana Prieto, "The Effect of the Time Profile of Unemployment Insurance Benefits on Exit from Unemployment," *CREST Working Paper* (2000), available at http://www.crest.fr. See as well their article "L'effet de l'allocation unique dégressive sur la reprise d'emploi," *Économie et statistique* 343 (2001): 3–28.

7. In fact, the data available show that the rates at which unemployed persons refuse job offers are very low and vary little. Thus, it is probably the job search that intensifies as the end of entitlement approaches.

8. J.-B. Séverac, "Le mouvement syndical," in *Encyclopédie socialiste syndicale et coopérative de l'Internationale ouvrière*, ed. [Adéodat Constant Adolphe] Compère-Morel (Paris: Aristide Quillet, 1913), p. 111. Most of the historical information given in this section is taken from this encyclopedia. The history of the system of unemployment insurance in France since 1884 is very well told in Christine Daniel and Carole Tuchszirer, *L'État face aux chômeurs* (Paris: Flammarion, 1999).

9. Séverac, "Le mouvement syndical," p. 115.

10. The analysis of the effects of unemployment insurance in Switzerland presented here relies on the work of Rafael Lalive, Jan Van Ours, and Josef

Zweimüller, as described in "The Effect of Benefit Sanctions on the Duration of Unemployment," *Journal of the European Economic Association* 3 (2005): 1386–1417.

11. This controlled experiment and its results are described in detail in the article by Peter Dolton and Donald O'Neill, "Unemployment Duration and the Restart Effect: Some Experimental Evidence," *Economic Journal* 106, no. 435 (March 1996): 387–400.

12. See D. Black, J. Smith, M. Berger, and B. Noel, "Is the Threat of Reemployment Services More Effective than the Services Themselves? Evidence from UI System Using Random Assignment," *American Economic Review* 98 (2003): 1313–1327.

13. See Jaap Abbring, Gerard Van den Berg, and Jan Van Ours, "The Effect of Unemployment Insurance Sanctions on the Transition Rate from Unemployment to Employment," *Economic Journal* 115 (2005): 602–630. There is not, at the moment of writing, a real consensus on the effects or the value of "profiling" unemployed persons by assigning each of them a score meant to reflect his capacity to find a new job with greater or less difficulty. The study of Black et al., "Is the Threat of Reemployment Services more Effective than the Services Themselves?" shows that the system of assistance and checking set up in Kentucky had practically no beneficial effect on the groups with the highest and lowest scores.

14. The protocol and the results of this controlled experiment are reported in Gerard Van den Berg and Bas Van der Klauw, "Counseling and Monitoring of Unemployed Workers: Theory and Evidence from a Controlled Social Experiment," working paper, Free University of Amsterdam, 2001.

15. For more details on the U.S. experiments, see Bruce Meyer, "Lessons from the U.S. Unemployment Insurance Experiments," *Journal of Economic Literature* 33 (1995): 91–131.

Chapter 6

1. A layoff is described as "economic" if the reasons for it have nothing to do with the person laid off, but derive solely from economic difficulties or technological changes the firm is undergoing. An economic layoff can be individual or collective. In France it is collective when it affects more than one wage-earner during a 30-day period. The procedures the firm must follow are more restrictive in the case of a collective layoff, especially if it affects more than 10 employees. The concept of "economic layoff" exists in several European countries but with variable definitions. It does not exist in the United States.

2. Readers will find a synthesis of this empirical research in John Addison and Paulino Teixeira, "The Economics of Employment Protection," *Journal of Labor Research* 24, no. 1 (2003): 85–129; and David Autor, John Donohue, and

Stewart Schwab, "The Costs of Wrongful-Discharge Laws," *NBER Working Paper* no. 9425 (2002), available at www.nber.org, and forthcoming in *Review of Economics and Statistics*.

3. This results from the negative impact of employment protection on job creation. Since employment protection has the effect of reducing both job destruction and job creation without affecting the unemployment rate significantly, unemployed persons have less chance of finding a new job, and this increases the average duration of unemployment.

4. Since employment protection tends to increase the duration of unemployment, it causes psychological wear and a waste of human capital; these can drive the unemployed to abandon the search for a job and so become inactive. Since the unemployment rate is not significantly affected by employment protection, in the end it is the employment rate that falls.

5. This is the finding of a number of studies. See Olivier Blanchard and Augustin Landier, "The Perverse Effect of Partial Labor Market Reform: Fixed-Term Contract in France," *Economic Journal* 112 (2002): 214–244; and Pierre Cahuc and Fabien Postel-Vinay, "Temporary Jobs, Employment Protection and Labor Market Performance," *Labour Economics* 9 (2002): 63–91.

6. See Patricia Anderson and Bruce Meyer, "The Effects of the Unemployment Insurance Payroll Tax on Wages, Employment, Claims and Denials," *Journal of Public Economics* 78 (2000): 81–106.

Chapter 7

1. See our own work, *Labor Economics* (Cambridge: MIT Press, 2004), ch. 2.

2. The OECD publishes *Education at a Glance/Regards sur l'éducation* at regular intervals. Data given here are taken from the edition for 2004. (Fuller information and long abstracts are available at http://www.oecd.org.)

3. *Education at a Glance*, 2004.

4. The study of Lance Lochner and Enrico Moretti, "The Effect of Education on Criminal Activity: Evidence from Prison Inmates, Arrests and Self-Reports," *American Economic Review* 94, no. 1 (2004): 155–189, looks at the United States over the period 1960 to 1980. It shows that having attended high school significantly increases the gains from education flowing to society as a whole. These social gains lie in the range of between 14 percent and 26 percent of the gains individuals derive from education as a result of the higher wages it makes possible.

5. This finding is published in Janett Currie and Enrico Moretti, "Mother's Education and the Intergenerational Transmission of Human Capital: Evidence from College Openings and Longitudinal Data," *Quarterly Journal of Economics* 118, no. 3 (2003): 1495–1532.

6. Eric Hanushek, John Kain, Jacob Markman, and Steven Rivkin, "Does Peer Ability Affect Student Achievement?," *Journal of Applied Econometrics* 18, no. 5 (2003): 527–544.

7. For example, many studies of the shipbuilding industry in the United States during World War II have shown that this type of externality contributed significantly to the rise in the productivity of labor in this industry during this period. See Rebecca Thornton and Peter Thompson, "Learning from Experience and Learning from Others: An Exploration of Learning and Spillovers in Wartime Shipbuilding," *American Economic Review* 91 (2001): 1350–1368.

8. The work of James Heckman, which has largely focused on the evaluation of public policies, was recognized by the award of the Nobel Prize for economics in 2002. The ground-breaking article of D. Rubin, "Estimating Causal Effects of Treatments in Randomized and Non-Randomized Studies," *Journal of Educational Psychology* 66 (1974): 688–701, focused on the evaluation of medical treatments.

9. The ideal solution to the problem of neutralizing the effects of characteristics not captured would be to set up a controlled experiment. For that, two groups of (let's say) 10,000 persons each would have to be drawn completely at random from the population of all unemployed persons older than 25 without a high school diploma. The test group would take the course, the control group would not. Comparison of the average life trajectories of these two groups would yield an indicator of the efficiency of the course. In the area of employment assistance this approach is seldom adopted, especially in Europe, and statisticians must work with real-world data and use the technique of matching. The Self-Sufficiency Project described in chapter 4 is such a controlled experiment carried out in Canada in the area of employment assistance.

10. The interested reader may consult the synthesis by James Heckman, Robert Lalonde, and John Smith, "The Economics and Econometrics of Active Labor Market Programs," in Ashenfelter and Card, eds., *Handbook of Labor Economics*, vol. 3A (1999), ch. 31, pp. 1865–2097.

11. See Heckman, Lalonde and Smith, "The Economics and Econometrics of Active Labor Market Programs."

12. See Dominique Goux and Éric Maurin, "Returns to Firm-Provided Training: Evidence from French Worker-Firm Matched Data," *Labour Economics* 7, no. 1 (2000): 1–20.

13. This finding is well-documented in Emmanuel Delame and Francis Kramarz, "Entreprises et formation continue," *Économie et prévision* 127 (1999): 63–82. The paper by Andrea Bassanini, Alison L. Booth, Giorgio Brunello, Maria De Paola, and Edwin Leuven, "Workplace Training in Europe," *IZA Discussion Paper* no. 1640 (2005), provides further evidence on this issue for European countries.

14. See the presentation by Greg Parks, "The High/Scope Perry Preschool Project," *Juvenile Justice Bulletin* (October 2000): 1–7, U.S. Department of

Justice, available at www.ncjrs.org/pdffiles1/ojjdp/181725.pdf. A full evaluation of this program is given in L. J. Schweinhart, J. Montie, Z. Xiang, W. S. Barnett, C. R. Belfield, and M. Nores, *Lifetime Effects: The High/Scope Perry Preschool Study through Age 40*, Monographs of the High/Scope Educational Research Foundation, 14 (Ypsilanti, MI: High/Scope Press, 2005).

15. See the OECD report *Starting Strong: Early Childhood Education and Care/Petite enfance, grands défis: Éducation et structures d'accueil*, published in 2001 (summaries and information about versions in other languages at www.oecd.org); and Pedro Carneiro and James Heckman, "Human Capital Policy," *NBER Working Paper* no. 9495 (February 2003); available at www.nber.org.

16. Carneiro and Heckman, "Human Capital Policy."

17. Joseph Tierney, Jean-Baldwin Grossman, and Nancy Resch, "Making a Difference: An Impact Study of Big Brothers Big Sisters," *Public Private Ventures* (2000), available at www.ppv.org/content/reports/makingadiff.html.

18. Carneiro and Heckman, "Human Capital Policy."

19. Jack Shonkoff and Deborah Phillips, *From Neurons to Neighborhoods: The Science of Early Childhood Development* (Washington, DC: National Academic Press, 2000). More generally, advances in neuroscience during the last 20 years have greatly improved our understanding of the processes of knowledge acquisition and personality formation, though much remains to be discovered in this field. The manual by Deric Bownds, *The Biology of Mind: Origins and Structures of Mind, Brain, and Consciousness* (Hoboken, NJ: John Wiley and Sons, 1999), offers an accessible and well-documented presentation of the principal findings of research on the brain. The OECD report *Understanding the Brain: Towards a New Learning Science* (2002) offers a synthesis of the applications of this research in the field of education, emphasizing their highly exploratory character.

20. On this point, and on many other aspects of the plasticity of the brain, see part two of Bownds, *The Biology of Mind*.

21. The linkages between social origin and educational outcomes in France are well illustrated in Claude Thélot and Louis-André Vallet, "La réduction des inégalités sociales devant l'école depuis le début du siècle," *Économie et statistique* 334 (2000): 3–32. Thélot and Vallet show that social origin profoundly influences educational outcomes, and emphasize as well that the education system was democratized during the course of the twentieth century. In addition to the generally longer duration of schooling, which automatically favors the accession of children of modest social background to study for higher degrees (except in the case of France's elite "grandes écoles"), there has also been a qualitative democratization of the education system, which also favors the social ascent of persons from modest social backgrounds, especially since the 1960s.

22. The precise effects of the respective contributions of income and parental educational level are not yet clearly established. See Éric Maurin, "The Impact of Parental Income on Early Schooling Transitions: A Re-Examination Using Data over Three Generations," *Journal of Public Economics* 85 (2002): 301–332; and Carneiro and Heckman, "Human Capital Policy."

23. Dominique Goux and Éric Maurin, "The Effect of Over-Crowded Housing on Children's Performance at School," CREST-INSEE 2001 (photocopy); forthcoming in *Journal of Public Economics*.

24. This result is confirmed in numerous studies carried out by clinicians, psychologists, and sociologists. These studies are reviewed in Goux and Maurin, "The Effect of Over-crowded Housing."

25. Readers may consult Erik Hanushek, "Publicly Provided Education," in A. J. Auerbach and M. Feldstein, eds., *Handbook of Public Economics*, vol. 4 (Amsterdam and New York: Elsevier Science, 2002), ch. 30, pp. 2045–2141. The author offers a synthesis of 376 published studies on the subject and shows clearly that outlays devoted to increasing the number of teachers per pupil, teachers' salaries, and expenditure per pupil yield, on average, no positively significant impact on the performance of pupils as measured by how they do in tests, or by their performance on the labor market.

26. We rely to a large extent on the synthesis of Carneiro and Heckman, "Human Capital Policy."

27. Roland Bénabou, Francis Kramarz, and Corinne Prost, "Zones d'éducation prioritaire: Quels moyens pour quels résultats?" *CREST Working Paper*, 2003; available at http://www.crest.fr/pageperso/dr/kramarz/articlezep 04112003.pdf. According to the authors, the financial resources invested do not translate into a significant improvement in the educational resources. Class size, the teacher-pupil ratio, and the qualifications and experience of the teachers remain in fact very close to what they were previously in institutions assigned to priority education zones. There is a fall in student numbers at these institutions, however, which may be explained by a stigmatization phenomenon, leading to reduced enrollment and more students leaving for other public or private schools, especially students from relatively privileged socio-economic backgrounds.

28. Goux and Maurin, "The Effect of Over-Crowded Housing on Children's Performance at School."

29. John Bughardt, Peter Shochet, Sheena McConnell, Terry Johnson, Mark Gritz, Steven Glazerman, John Homrighausen, and Russell Jackson, "Does Job Corps Work?" 2001, available at http://wdr.doleta.gov.

30. Carneiro and Heckman, "Human Capital Policy."

31. John Rawls, *A Theory of Justice*, rev. ed. (Cambridge, Mass.: Belknap Press of Harvard University Press, 1999; first published 1971).

Chapter 8

1. According to the definitions of the OECD, policies to assist employment belong in the category of "active" labor market policy, as opposed to "passive" policies that do not seek to increase the employability of individuals, but simply try to make sure that the material situation of jobless workers does not deteriorate drastically. Passive policies principally include arrangements for early retirement and for the payment of unemployment insurance benefits. In practice, the boundary between active and passive policies turns out to be porous, to say the least. For example, measures to give job-seekers supportive care and attention, which we analyzed in chapter 5, fall into the category of active policy, whereas unemployment insurance falls into that of passive policy. For this reason, we generally try to avoid using the terms "active" and "passive" to characterize employment policies, but they do crop up in the literature, and so are sometimes used in the text and notes of this chapter.

2. See Heckman, Lalonde, and Smith, "The Economics and Econometrics of Active Labor Market Programs."

3. The public job creation programs born in the 1970s, especially under the umbrella of the Comprehensive Employment and Training Act (CETA) of 1973, were gradually restricted to persons in difficulty before being abolished in 1983 by the administration of Ronald Reagan. On this topic, for a comparative study of several OECD countries, see Melvin Brodsky, "Public-Service Employment Programs in Selected OECD Countries," *Monthly Labor Review* 123, no. 10 (2000): 31–41.

4. These figures come from table H of the statistical annex of the OECD's *Employment Outlook*, July 2005. To arrive at totals of aid to employment, we have added up expenditure on training, employment incentives, and direct job creation.

5. Draft finance bill, 2003, annex 6, p. 46, available at www.minefi.gouv.fr.

6. Information report no 1781, presented by Didier Migaud before the National Assembly in 1999, annex 3, p. 38; emphasis added.

7. Adequate methodology aims to eliminate "selectivity bias." See the subsection "How to evaluate public policies on employment?" in chapter 7.

8. Barbara Sianesi, "Differential Effects of Swedish Active Labour Market Programmes for Unemployed Adults during the 1990s," research document of IFAU (Swedish Institute for Labor Market Policy Evaluation), no. 5, 2002, available at www.ifau.se. Barbara Sianesi is a researcher at the Institute for Fiscal Studies, London.

9. In addition, participation in these programs enabled one to prolong one's entitlement to unemployment insurance, which might also have caused job searches to be conducted less vigorously. This provision was suppressed in February 2001.

10. Lars Calmfors, Anders Forslund, and Maria Henström, "Does Active Labor Market Policy Work? Lessons from the Swedish Experiences," *Swedish*

Economic Policy Review 85 (2001): 61–124. Lars Calmfors is professor of international economics at the Institute for International Economic Studies at the University of Stockholm. Anders Forslund and Maria Henström are researchers at IFAU (the Swedish Institute for Labor Market Policy Evaluation).

11. Michael Gerfin and Michael Lechner, "A Microeconometric Evaluation of the Active Labour Market Policy in Switzerland," *Economic Journal* 112 (482) (2002): 854–893. Michael Lechner is professor of econometrics at the University of St. Gallen and director of SIAW, the Swiss Institute for International Economics and Applied Economic Research. Michael Gerfin is professor of economics at the faculty of social sciences, University of Bern.

12. Thomas Brodaty, Bruno Crépon, and Denis Fougère, "Using Kernel Matching Estimators to Evaluate Alternative Youth Employment Programs: Evidence from France, 1986–1988," in M. Lechner and F. Pfeiffer, eds., *Econometric Evaluations of Labour Market Policies* (Heidelberg: Physica Verlag, 2001), 85–124. See as well Denis Fougère, Francis Kramarz, and Thierry Magnac, "Youth Employment Policies in France," *European Economic Review* 44 (2000): 928–942. This article sums up research assessing the employment policies adopted in France to help young people. In it readers will find confirmation of the main results we state in this section.

13. Calmfors, Forslund, and Henström, "Does Active Labor Market Policy Work?"

14. The global effects of fiscality on employment are not yet well understood. No study shows that a rise in payroll taxes decreases employment, but certain studies do conclude that the amount of payroll taxes exerts no significant effect on the level of employment. See the well-documented article by Francesco Daveri and Guido Tabellini, "Unemployment, Growth and Taxation in Industrial Countries," *Economic Policy* (April 2000): 49–104.

15. All the examples put forward in this section are hypothetical and are meant to illustrate the economic mechanisms of substitution and complementarity. Any resemblance to actually existing programs is fortuitous.

16. See, for example, Yann Algan, Pierre Cahuc, and André Zylberberg, "Public Employment and Labour Market Performances," *Economic Policy* 34 (April 2002): 8–65, which finds that the creation of 100 public-sector jobs destroyed around 150 private-sector jobs on average, in 17 OECD countries between 1960 and 2000. Thus, this study highlights very strong crowding-out effects.

Select Bibliography

Abbring, Jaap, Gerard Van den Berg, and Jan Van Ours. "The Effect of Unemployment Insurance Sanctions on the Transition Rate from Unemployment to Employment." *Economic Journal* 115 (2005): 602–630.

Abowd, John, Patrick Corbel, and Francis Kramarz. "The Entry and Exit of Workers and the Growth of Employment." *Review of Economics and Statistics* 81, no. 2 (1999): 170–187.

Abowd, John, Francis Kramarz, David Margolis, and Thomas Philippon. "The Tail of Two Countries: Minimum Wage and Employment in France and the United States." *IZA Discussion Paper* no. 203 (2000). Available at www.iza.org.

Acemoglu, Daron, and Robert Shimer. "Productivity Gains from Unemployment Insurance." *European Economic Review* 44 (2000): 1115–1125.

Addison, John, and Paulino Teixeira. "The Economics of Employment Protection." *Journal of Labor Research* 24, no. 1 (2003): 85–129.

Aghion, Philippe, and Peter Howitt. *Endogenous Growth Theory.* Cambridge: MIT Press, 1998.

Algan, Yann, Pierre Cahuc, and André Zylberberg. "Public Employment and Labour Market Performances." *Economic Policy* 34 (April 2002): 8–65.

Anderson, Patricia, and Bruce Meyer. "The Effects of the Unemployment Insurance Payroll Tax on Wages, Employment, Claims and Denials." *Journal of Public Economics* 78 (2000): 81–106.

Angrist, Joshua, and Adriana Kugler. "Productive or Counter-Productive? Labor Market Institutions and the Effect of Immigration on European Union Natives." *IZA Discussion Paper* no. 433 (2002). Available at http://www.iza.org, and published in *Economic Journal* 113 (2003): F302–F331.

Anne, Denis, and Yannick L'Horty. "Transferts sociaux locaux et retour à l'emploi." *Économie et statistique* 357–358 (2002): 49–71.

Ashenfelter, Orley, and David Card, eds. *Handbook of Labor Economics.* Vol. 3 (3 parts: 3A, 3B, 3C). Amsterdam and New York: Elsevier Science, 1999.

Ashenfelter, Orley, and Richard Layard, eds. *Handbook of Labor Economics.* Vol. 1. Amsterdam and New York: Elsevier Science, 1986.

Ashenfelter, Orley, and Richard Layard, eds. *Handbook of Labor Economics.* Vol. 2. Amsterdam and New York: Elsevier Science, 1986.

Autor, David, John Donohue, and Stewart Schwab. "The Costs of Wrongful-Discharge Laws." *NBER Working Paper* no. 9425 (2002). Available at www.nber.org, and forthcoming in *Review of Economics and Statistics.*

Bairoch, Paul. *Victoires et déboires: Histoire économique et sociale du monde du XVIᵉ siècle à nos jours.* Paris: Gallimard, 1997. 3 vols.

Bartelsman, Eric, Stefano Scarpetta, and Fabiano Schivardi. "Comparative Analysis of Firm Demographics and Survival: Micro-level Evidence for the OECD Countries." Research paper of the OECD economics department, no. 348 (2003). Available at http://ideas.repec.org/p/oecd/oecdec/348.html.

Bassanini, Andrea, Alison L. Booth, Giorgio Brunello, Maria De Paola, and Edwin Leuven. "Workplace Training in Europe." *IZA Discussion Paper* no. 1640 (2005).

Bénabou, Roland, Francis Kramarz, and Corinne Prost. "Zones d'éducation prioritaire: Quels moyens pour quels résultats?" *CREST Working Paper,* 2003. Available at http://www.crest.fr/pageperso/dr/kramarz/articlezep 04112003.pdf.

Billger, Sherrilyn, and Kevin Hallock. "Mass Layoffs and CEO Turnover." *Industrial Relations* 44, no. 3 (2005): 463–489.

Black, D., J. Smith, M. Berger, and B. Noel. "Is the Threat of Reemployment Services More Effective than the Services Themselves? Evidence from UI System Using Random Assignment." *American Economic Review* 98 (2003): 1313–1327.

Blanchard, Olivier, and Augustin Landier. "The Perverse Effect of Partial Labor Market Reform: Fixed-Term Contract in France." *Economic Journal* 112 (2002): 214–244.

Blank, Rebecca. "Evaluating Welfare Reform in the United States." *Journal of Economic Literature* 40, no. 4 (December 2002): 1105–1166.

Blundell, Richard. "Welfare Reform for Low Income Workers." *Oxford Economic Papers* 53, no. 2 (2001): 189–214.

Blundell, Richard, Mike Brewer, and Andrew Shephard. "Evaluating the Labour Market Impact of Working Families' Tax Credit Using Difference-in-Differences." Report of the Institute for Fiscal Studies (2005). Available at www.hmrc.gov.uk/research/ifs-did.pdf.

Boissonnat, Jean. *La fin du chômage.* Paris: Calmann-Levy, 2001.

Borjas, George. "The Economic Analysis of Immigration." In Ashenfelter and Card, eds., *Handbook of Labor Economics* 3A (1999): 1697–1760.

Borjas, George. "The Labor Demand Curve Is Downward Sloping: Reexamining the Impact of Immigration on the Labor Market." *Quarterly Journal of Economics* 118 (2003): 1135–1174.

Bownds, Deric. *The Biology of Mind: Origins and Structures of Mind, Brain, and Consciousness.* Hoboken, NJ: John Wiley and Sons, 1999.

Brodaty, Thomas, Bruno Crépon, and Denis Fougère. "Using Kernel Matching Estimators to Evaluate Alternative Youth Employment Programs: Evidence from France, 1986–1988." In M. Lechner and F. Pfeiffer, eds., *Econometric Evaluations of Labour Market Policies*, pp. 85–124. Heidelberg: Physica Verlag, 2001.

Brodsky, Melvin. "Public-Service Employment Programs in Selected OECD Countries." *Monthly Labor Review* 123, no. 10 (2000): 31–41.

Brown, David, and John Earl. "Job Reallocation and Productivity Growth under Alternative Economic Systems and Policies: Evidence from the Soviet Transition." *Working Paper* no. 514 (2002), William Davidson Institute, University of Michigan. Available at www.wdi.bus.umich.edu.

Bughardt, John, Peter Shochet, Sheena McConnell, Terry Johnson, Mark Gritz, Steven Glazerman, John Homrighausen, and Russell Jackson. "Does Job Corps Work?" (2001). Available at http://wdr.doleta.gov.

Burniaux, Jean-Marc, Romain Duval, and Florence Jaumotte. "Coping with Ageing: A Dynamic Approach to Quantify the Impact of Alternative Policy Options on Future Labour Supply in OECD Countries." *OECD Economic Department Working Paper* no. 371 (2003). Available at www.oecd.org.

Caballero, Ricardo, and Mohamad Hammour. "On the Timing and Efficiency of Creative Destruction." *Quarterly Journal of Economics* 111, no. 3 (1996): 805–852.

Cahuc, Pierre. "À quoi sert la prime pour l'emploi?" *Revue française d'économie* 16 (January 2002): 3–61.

Cahuc, Pierre. "Les expériences françaises de réduction du temps de travail: Moins d'emplois et plus d'inégalités." *Revue française d'économie* 15, no. 3 (January 2001): 141–166.

Cahuc, Pierre, and Pierre Granier, eds. *La réduction du temps de travail: Une solution pour l'emploi?* Paris: Economica, 1997.

Cahuc, Pierre, and Fabien Postel-Vinay. "Temporary Jobs, Employment Protection and Labor Market Performance." *Labour Economics* 9 (2002): 63–91.

Cahuc, Pierre, and André Zylberberg. *Labor Economics.* Cambridge: MIT Press, 2004.

Calmfors, Lars, Anders Forslund, and Maria Henström. "Does Active Labor Market Policy Work? Lessons from the Swedish Experiences." *Swedish Economic Policy Review* 85 (2001): 61–124.

Card, David. "The Impact of the Mariel Boatlift on the Miami Labor Market," *Industrial and Labor Relations Review* 43 (1990): 245–257.

Card, David, and John DiNardo. "Do Immigrant Inflows Lead to Native Outflows?" *American Economic Review, Papers and Proceedings* 90 (2000): 361–367.

Card, David, and Alan Krueger. "Minimum Wages and Employment: A Case Study of the Fast-Food Industry in New Jersey and Pennsylvania." *American Economic Review* 84 (1994): 772–793.

Card, David, and Alan Krueger. "Minimum Wages and Employment: A Case Study of the Fast-Food Industry in New Jersey and Pennsylvania: Reply." *American Economic Review* 90 (2000): 1397–1420.

Card, David, and Alan Krueger. *Myth and Measurement: The New Economics of the Minimum Wage*. Princeton: Princeton University Press, 1995.

Carneiro, Pedro, and James Heckman. "Human Capital Policy." *NBER Working Paper* no. 9495 (February 2003). Available at www.nber.org.

Cette, Gilbert, and Dominique Taddei. *Réduire la durée du travail*. Paris: Le Livre de Poche, 1997. Series "Réferences."

Comparative Civilian Labor Force Statistics, 10 Countries, 1960–2004. Bureau of Labor Statistics (BLS) of the U.S. Department of Labor, Office of Productivity and Technology, 13 May 2005. Available at www.bls.gov/fls/flslforc.pdf.

Contensou, François, and Radu Vranceanu. *Working Time: Theory and Policy Implications*. Cheltenham, UK: Edward Elgar Publishing, 2000.

Corbin, Alain, ed. *L'avènement des loisirs*. Paris: Aubier, 1995.

Crépon, Bruno, and Rosenn Desplatz. "Une nouvelle évaluation des effets des allègements de charges sociales sur les bas salaires." *Économie et statistique* 348 (2001): 1–24. Available in English as "Evaluating the Effects of Payroll Tax Subsidies for Low-Wage Workers," at www.crest.fr/pageperso/dr/crepon/crepon_angl.htm.

Crépon, Bruno, and Francis Kramarz. "Employed 40 Hours or Not-Employed 39: Lessons from the 1982 Workweek Reduction in France." *Journal of Political Economy* 110 (2002): 1355–1389.

Crépon, Bruno, and Francis Kramarz. "Le passage aux 39 heures en 1982." *Économie internationale: La revue du CEPII* 85 (2000): 85–94.

Currie, Janett, and Enrico Moretti. "Mother's Education and the Intergenerational Transmission of Human Capital: Evidence from College Openings and Longitudinal Data." *Quarterly Journal of Economics* 118, no. 3 (2003): 1495–1532.

Daniel, Christine, and Carole Tuchszirer. *L'État face aux chômeurs*. Paris: Flammarion, 1999.

Daveri, Francesco, and Guido Tabellini. "Unemployment, Growth and Taxation in Industrial Countries." *Economic Policy* (April 2000): 49–104.

Davis, Steven, Jason Faberman, and John Haltiwanger. "The Flow Approach to Labor Markets: New Data Sources, Micro-Macro Links and the Recent Downturn." *IZA Discussion Paper* no. 1639 (2005). Available at www.iza.org.

Davis, Steven, and John Haltiwanger. "Gross Job Flows." In Ashenfelter and Card, eds., *Handbook of Labor Economics*, vol. 3B (1999), ch. 41, pp. 2711–2805.

Delame, Emmanuel, and Francis Kramarz. "Entreprises et formation continue." *Économie et prévision* 127 (1999): 63–82.

Dolton, Peter, and Donald O'Neill. "Unemployment Duration and the Restart Effect: Some Experimental Evidence." *Economic Journal* 106, no. 435 (March 1996): 387–400.

Dormont, Brigitte, Denis Fougère, and Ana Prieto. "L'effet de l'allocation unique dégressive sur la reprise d'emploi." *Économie et statistique* 343 (2001): 3–28.

Dormont, Brigitte, Denis Fougère, and Ana Prieto. "The Effect of the Time Profile of Unemployment Insurance Benefits on Exit from Unemployment." *CREST Working Paper* (2000). Available at http://www.crest.fr.

Duhautois, Richard. "Les réallocations d'emplois en France sont-elles en phase avec le cycle?" *Économie et statistique* 351 (2002).

Dustmann, Christian, Tim Hatton, and Ian Preston. "The Labour Market Effects of Immigration." *Economic Journal* 115 (2005): F297–F299.

Education at a Glance / Regards sur l'éducation. OECD, 2004.

Ellwood, David. "Anti-poverty Policy for Families in the Next Century: From Welfare to Work and Worries." *Journal of Economic Perspectives* 14, no. 1 (winter 2000): 187–198.

Employment Outlook. OECD, July 2005.

Farber, Henry, and Kevin Hallock. "Have Employment Reductions Become Good News for Shareholders? The Effect of Job Loss Announcements on Stock Prices, 1970–1997." *NBER Working Paper* no. W795 (August 1999).

Feldstein, Martin. "The Effect of Marginal Tax Rates on Taxable Income: A Panel Study of the 1986 Tax Reform Act." *Journal of Political Economy* 103 (1995): 551–572.

Forrester, Viviane. *The Economic Horror.* Cambridge, U.K.: Polity Press, 1999. Originally published in French, 1996.

Foster, Lucia, John Haltiwanger, and C.-J. Krisan. "Aggregate Productivity Growth: Lessons from Microeconomic Evidence." In E. Dean, M. Harper, and C. Hulten, eds., *New Developments in Productivity Analysis.* Chicago: University of Chicago Press, 2001.

Foster, Lucia, John Haltiwanger, and C.-J. Krisan. "The Link between Aggregate and Micro Productivity Growth: Evidence from Retail Trade." *NBER Working Paper* no. 9120, August 2002. Available at http://www.nber.org/papers/w9120.

Fougère, Denis, Francis Kramarz, and Thierry Magnac. "Youth Employment Policies in France." *European Economic Review* 44 (2000): 928–942.

Freeman, Richard, and Remcom Oostendorp. "Wages around the World: Pay across Occupations and Countries." *NBER Working Paper* no. 8058 (2000). Available at www.nber.org.

Gerfin, Michael, and Michael Lechner. "A Microeconometric Evaluation of the Active Labour Market Policy in Switzerland." *Economic Journal* 112, no. 482 (2002): 854–893.

Goux, Dominique, and Éric Maurin. "The Effect of Over-Crowded Housing on Children's Performance at School." CREST-INSEE 2001 (photocopy). Forthcoming in *Journal of Public Economics*.

Goux, Dominique, and Éric Maurin. "Returns to Firm-Provided Training: Evidence from French Worker-Firm Matched Data." *Labour Economics* 7, no. 1 (2000): 1–20.

Greenwood, J., and J.-P. Voyer. "Experimental Evidence on the Use of Earnings Supplements as a Strategy to 'Make Work Pay.'" *OECD Economic Studies* 31 (2000): 52–79.

Gruber, Jon, and Emmanuel Saez. "The Elasticity of Taxable Income: Evidence and Implications." *Journal of Public Economics* 84 (2002): 1–32.

Guimbert, Stéphane, and François Lévy-Bruhl. "La situation de l'emploi en France face aux échanges internationaux." *Économie et prévision* 152–153 (January–March 2002): 189–206.

Haltiwanger, John, and Milan Vodopivec. "Gross Worker and Job Flows in a Transition Economy: An Analysis of Estonia." Working paper, University of Maryland (2000).

Hanushek, Erik. "Publicly Provided Education." In A. J. Auerbach and M. Feldstein, eds., *Handbook of Public Economics*, vol. 4: 2045–2141. Amsterdam and New York: Elsevier Science, 2002.

Hanushek, Eric, John Kain, Jacob Markman, and Steven Rivkin. "Does Peer Ability Affect Student Achievement?" *Journal of Applied Econometrics* 18, no. 5 (2003): 527–544.

Heckman, James, Robert Lalonde, and John Smith. "The Economics and Econometrics of Active Labor Market Programs." In Ashenfelter and Card, eds., *Handbook of Labor Economics*, vol. 3A (1999): 1865–2097.

Hunt, Jennifer. "Has Work-Sharing Worked in Germany?" *Quarterly Journal of Economics* 114 (1999): 117–148.

Hunt, Jennifer. "The Impact of the 1962 Repatriates from Algeria on the French Labor Market." *Industrial and Labor Relations Review* 45 (1992): 556–572.

Immervoll, Herwig, Henrik Kleven, Claus Kreiner, and Emmanuel Saez. "Welfare Reform in European Countries: A Micro Simulation Analysis." Forthcoming in *Economic Journal*.

Lalive, Rafael, Jan Van Ours, and Josef Zweimüller. "The Effect of Benefit Sanctions on the Duration of Unemployment." *Journal of the European Economic Association* 3 (2005): 1386–1417.

Laroque, Guy, and Bernard Salanié. "Labor Market Institutions and Employment in France." *Journal of Applied Econometrics* 17, no. 1 (2002): 25–48.

Lindsey, Lawrence. "Individual Taxpayer Response to Tax Cuts 1982–1984, with Implications for the Revenue Maximizing Tax Rate." *Journal of Public Economics* 33 (1987): 173–206.

Lochner, Lance, and Enrico Moretti. "The Effect of Education on Criminal Activity: Evidence from Prison Inmates, Arrests and Self-Reports." *American Economic Review* 94, no. 1 (2004): 155–189.

Manning, Alan. *Monopsony in Motion: Imperfect Competition in Labor Markets.* Princeton: Princeton University Press, 2003.

Maurin, Éric. "The Impact of Parental Income on Early Schooling Transitions: A Re-Examination Using Data over Three Generations." *Journal of Public Economics* 85 (2002): 301–332.

McMillan, John. *Reinventing the Bazaar.* New York: Norton, 2002.

Meyer, Bruce. "Lessons from the U.S. Unemployment Insurance Experiments." *Journal of Economic Literature* 33 (1995): 91–131.

Meyer, Bruce, Kip Viscusi, and David Durbin. "Workers' Compensation and Injury Duration: Evidence from a Natural Experiment." *American Economic Review* 85 (June 1995): 322–340.

Michalopoulos, Charles, ed. *Making Work Pay: Final Report on the Self-Sufficiency Project for Long Term Welfare Recipients.* The Social Research and Demonstration Corporation, Canada, July 2002. Available at www.srdc.org/english/publications/SSP54.htm.

Michalopoulos, Charles, Philipp Robin, and David Card. "When Financial Incentives Pay for Themselves: Evidence from a Randomized Social Experiment for Welfare Recipients." *Journal of Public Economics* 89 (2005): 5–29.

Michéa, Jean-Claude. *Impasse Adam Smith: Brèves remarques sur l'impossibilité de dépasser le capitalisme sur sa gauche.* Paris: Éditions Climats, 2002.

Minc, Alain. *La France de l'an 2000.* Paris: Odile Jacob, 1994.

Mortensen, Dale. *Wage Dispersion: Why Are Similar People Paid Differently?* Cambridge: MIT Press, 2003.

Neumark, David, and William Wascher. "Minimum Wages and Employment: A Case Study of the Fast-Food Industry in New Jersey and Pennsylvania: Comment." *American Economic Review* 90 (2000): 1363–1393.

Parks, Greg. "The High-Scope Perry Preschool Project." *Juvenile Justice Bulletin*, (October 2000): 1–7, U.S. Department of Justice. Available at www.ncjrs.org/pdffiles1/ojjdp/181725.pdf.

Piketty, Thomas. "Les hauts revenus face aux modifications des taux marginaux supérieurs de l'impôt sur le revenu en France, 1970–1996." *Économie et prévision* 138–139 (1999): 25–60.

Piketty, Thomas. "Income Inequality in France, 1901–1998." *Journal of Political Economy* 111, no. 5 (2003): 1004–1042.

Piketty, Thomas. "L'impact des incitations financières au travail sur les comportements individuels: Une estimation pour le cas français." *Économie et prévision* 132–133 (January–March 1998): 1–36.

Réduction du temps du travail: Les enseignements de l'observation. Report of the commission headed by Henri Rouilleault. Paris: Documentation française, 2001.

Rubin, D. "Estimating Causal Effects of Treatments in Randomized and Non-Randomized Studies." *Journal of Educational Psychology* 66 (1974): 688–701.

Sauvy, Alfred. *La machine et le chômage.* Paris: Dunod, 1980.

Scarpetta, Stefano, Philip Hemmings, Thierry Tressel, and Jaejoon Woo. "The Role of Policy and Institutions for Productivity and Firm Dynamics: Evidence from Micro and Industry Data." *Working Paper* no. 329 (2002), OECD Economics Department. Available at www.oecd.org/eco.

Schumpeter, Joseph. *Capitalism, Socialism, and Democracy.* 6th edition with a new introduction by Tom Bottomore. London and Boston: Unwin Paperbacks, 1987; first published in 1942.

Schweinhart, L. J., J. Montie, Z. Xiang, W. S. Barnett, C. R. Belfield, and M. Nores. *Lifetime Effects: The High/Scope Perry Preschool Study through Age 40.* Monographs of the High/Scope Educational Research Foundation, 14. Ypsilanti, MI: High/Scope Press, 2005.

Sen, Amartya. *Development as Freedom.* New York: Alfred A. Knopf, 1999.

Séverac, J.-B. "Le mouvement syndical." In [Adéodat Constant Adolphe] Compère-Morel, ed., *Encyclopédie socialiste syndicale et coopérative de l'Internationale ouvrière.* Paris: Aristide Quillet, 1913.

Shonkoff, Jack, and Deborah Phillips. *From Neurons to Neighborhoods: The Science of Early Childhood Development.* Washington, DC: National Academic Press, 2000.

Sianesi, Barbara. "Differential Effects of Swedish Active Labour Market Programmes for Unemployed Adults during the 1990s." Research document of IFAU (Swedish Institute for Labor Market Policy Evaluation), no. 5, 2002. Available at www.ifau.se.

Starting Strong: Early Childhood Education and Care / Petite enfance, grands défis: Éducation et structures d'accueil. OECD, 2001.

Stigler, George. "The Economics of Minimum Wage Legislation." *American Economic Review* 36 (1946): 358–365.

Thélot, Claude, and Louis-André Vallet. "La réduction des inégalités sociales devant l'école depuis le début du siècle." *Économie et statistique* 334 (2000): 3–32.

Thornton, Rebecca, and Peter Thompson. "Learning from Experience and Learning from Others: An Exploration of Learning and Spillovers in Wartime Shipbuilding." *American Economic Review* 91 (2001): 1350–1368.

Tierney, Joseph, Jean-Baldwin Grossman, and Nancy Resch. "Making a Difference: An Impact Study of Big Brothers Big Sisters." *Public Private Ventures* (2000). Available at www.ppv.org/content/reports/makingadiff.html.

Understanding the Brain: Towards a New Learning Science. OECD, 2002.

Van den Berg, Gerard, and Bas Van der Klauw. "Counseling and Monitoring of Unemployed Workers: Theory and Evidence from a Controlled Social Experiment." Working paper, Free University of Amsterdam, 2001.

Zanda, Jean-Louis. "Les employeurs qui rencontrent des difficultés pour embaucher." *Les Cahiers de l'observatoire de l'ANPE* (March 2001): 27–52.

Index